BOATING EMERGENCIES

BOATING
EMERGENCIES

RAPID RESPONSE HANDBOOK

CAPTAIN RAMI GEFFNER, M.D.

Imar Publishing

ISBN (Paperback): 979-8-9991712-3-8
ISBN (eBook): 979-8-9991712-4-5

Cover photo by St. John's County Fire Rescue. Used with permission.

Cover design and interior formatting by the Aaxel Author Group

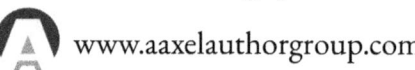 www.aaxelauthorgroup.com

To my entire family and fellow boaters

"Always prepare for the worst, and hope for the best!"
Thank you all for your love, support,
passion and inspiration.

Contents

DISCLAIMER

It is important for all my readers to know that before partaking in this book, you are agreeing to the following:

"While every effort has been made to ensure the accuracy and reliability of the information presented in this book, the author and publisher make no representations or warranties, express or implied, regarding its completeness or suitability for any particular purpose. This book is intended for informational purposes only, and readers are encouraged to exercise their own judgment and, where appropriate, seek professional advice before making decisions based on its content. The author assumes no responsibility for any consequences that may arise from the use of this material."

In no event shall Rami Geffner or anyone associated with the author to be liable for any direct, indirect, incidental, special exemplary, or consequential damages (including, but not limited to, procurement of substitute goods or services: loss of use, data, or profits; or business interruptions) however caused and on any theory of liability, whether in contract, strict liability, or tort (including negligence or otherwise) arising in any way out of the use of this book or its product, even if advised of the possibility of such damage. This limitation shall apply to claims of personal injury to the extent permitted by law.

The main reason for the above disclaimer is the nature of the complexity, dangers which are inherent in the challenges that accompany every boater, sea captain, crew and passengers. What worked yesterday may not work the next day due to the changes and circumstances that accompany each voyage. There are always indeterminable changes not only in the waterways but also on every boat.

PREFACE

My motivation for creating the *Quick Reference Guide to Boating Emergencies* was specifically to provide boaters with accessible, practical advice during critical moments. This concise handbook is directly inspired by the comprehensive resource, *Guide to Boating Emergencies*. While the original text offers extensive, detailed explanations ideal for thorough study and preparation, my intention with this quick reference version is to deliver immediate, easy-to-follow steps during urgent situations when every second counts.

Understanding that emergencies at sea require swift decision-making and clear action steps, I've distilled essential information into a straightforward, user-friendly format. Readers can quickly locate critical instructions and best practices without navigating extensive background details. This streamlined approach ensures that even under stress, boaters have rapid access to life-saving advice.

However, I strongly encourage boaters also to obtain and study the detailed companion book, *Guide to Boating Emergencies*. The importance of owning this more extensive resource cannot be overstated. It provides in-depth knowledge, background information, preventative measures, and comprehensive explanations that significantly enhance your understanding and preparedness for boating emergencies. Possessing both the quick reference guide for immediate action and the detailed companion for preparation and training creates a robust safety foundation, ultimately helping to prevent emergencies and manage them effectively should they occur.

My logic for creating this quick reference guide, supported by the detailed companion, is straightforward: clarity, brevity, and immediate usability significantly enhance safety and outcomes during emergencies, while comprehensive preparation and knowledge from the detailed guide ensure boaters are fully equipped for all situations.

FOREWORD

My passion for the sea started when I was young and grew from the moment I bought my first boat. As passion grew, so did the number and size of my boats. Within a few years, I was in command of my own fleet of boats. It all began with center consoles—ranging from single to triple outboard engines—followed by sport fishing boats, as described in my book *How to Buy Your First Boat*, and eventually led to a sixty-foot powered catamaran, which I had the privilege of chronicling in *The Intracoastal Voyage of the Sea Scape*. In *The Intracoastal Voyage of the Sea Scape*, I included maps describing my journey, culture and history of the trip, which took the boat through the longest man-made channel in the United States, the Intracoastal Waterway. The Intracoastal Waterway represents a network of canals, rivers, bays, and inlets that connect these waterways to the Atlantic Ocean and the Gulf coasts of the

United States. Even then, as I navigated through these waterways and oceans, having had the credentials of a sea captain for many years, I too ran into boating emergencies. **Murphy's Law says, "Anything that can go wrong will go wrong."** The tendency for the unexpected is always there, and because of this, we should **"Always be prepared for the worst and hope for the best."**

Over the years, I've had the privilege of learning and hearing from fellow boaters about their unfortunate experiences with regard to boating emergencies. Some were professional boat captains; others were just ordinary pleasure boaters who loved boating. Their experiences, along with my own, inspired me to write this book.

One conversation that I remember particularly touched my heart and truly inspired me. This person worked with BoatUS and, while sharing her thoughts with me, said that their office receives a lot of calls from boaters who run into boating emergencies. Even though their office is quite capable and equipped to handle most calls, they still face significant calls that they are less prepared to handle. The calls range from issues of mechanical failure to groundings, capsizing, health-related emergencies, weather emergencies and a bunch of others. Yet, despite their expertise and know-how, they sometimes lack the resources or experience to handle these calls. In addition, these distress calls coming into their office are far away in the distance. She explained to me that they would appreciate a good reference book that dealt exclusively with boating emergencies. Her desire from that day on became my inspiration, and this book was born from her inspiration as well as from those who have shared their experiences with me.

I hope this book will serve as a reference guide for those who want to learn and know more, especially in times of trouble. "An ounce of prevention is worth a pound of cure." As a reference book, I recommend keeping it close at hand for those moments when a quick guide is needed. The lady I spoke with at BoatUS admitted that she knew of no such book and that it was extremely necessary.

I too thought a book like this would be very helpful in acquainting oneself with potential issues before an impending emergency arises. Familiarity with the topics in this book is essential, as it can help reduce emotional reactions during emergencies by offering a clear, accessible reference. When used thoughtfully, meticulously, and in a step-by-step manner, it will serve as a reliable guide in emergency situations.

This book is as much about what to do as it is about what not to do and how to avoid that which could result in bad outcomes. It is also about readiness and preparation essential for avoiding and handling boating emergencies.

My motivation for writing this book was to share knowledge gained to help others. I would like to educate and help all those boaters who may one day face an unfortunate event.

I believe all boaters are bound by a shared love for the sea, a connection that transcends geography and brings us together like an unspoken brotherhood. Feeling deeply connected through our shared passion for boating, I am genuinely excited to share this book with you. It's filled with essential insights about boating emergencies, crafted to empower you with the knowledge and confidence you will need to achieve the best possible outcomes—because your safety and preparedness matter most to me. Anyone who would like to share and add to our experience and knowledge in any way should be in touch with me. I can always be reached at rami@ramigeffner.com or go to my website at ramigeffner.com.

Experience is what you get when
you don't get what you want.

Always be prepared for the worst
and hope for the best!

The outcome and results of managing any boating emergency depend on the level of skill and knowledge that one acquires. So let's get started.

Having the parts, tools, knowledge and foresight makes one better prepared to deal with stressful events that take place. Allow me to begin by presenting a couple of boating emergencies that I had to personally face.

I was leaving Fort Lauderdale in late May, heading to New Jersey. The day was very windy with gusts of 25-30 knots an hour, with rough seas approximately 4-6 feet. About an hour and a half later, while piloting the boat, I saw a red flashing light come on, which was my bilge alarm warning light. It flashed for a split second and disappeared. Initially I dismissed it, thinking that it was the result of rough seas. I thought a splash of the ocean water entered the pontoon within the engine room, causing this. Nothing too unusual. Not being overly concerned, I dismissed it until a second flashing red light came on for a split second again. Now I became a bit more suspicious and somewhat concerned. We definitely needed to check this out now. The Sea Scape was two miles off the Jupiter inlet in the Atlantic Ocean when this happened. I asked my first mate to go downstairs and peek into the engine room, just to check it out, never really fearing any disasters but rather doing this to reassure our safety. We did not have any cameras in the pontoon where the engine room was located. My first mate proceeded downstairs, and when she reached the midlevel of the ship and popped the hatch open leading to the engine room, she was extremely surprised.

A few minutes had passed since she had left the fly bridge to get to the stern starboard pontoon. I had not heard any alarms going off or communication from her. However, she ran up the stairs, almost holding her breath, and entered the bridge with the utmost trepidation and looking quite pale. As our eyes met, I knew that something was wrong. In a voice showing as much restraint as she could bear, for fear of letting out an uncontrollable scream, she said loud and clear, "We have a problem. There is seawater entering the pontoon and the bilge pump cannot keep up with the amount coming in." The boat was taking on a very significant amount of water. It soon became evident that we not only had a problem, but that the problem was significant and dangerous. A desperate situation. I pulled back on the throttle and slowed down the boat, trying not to bring the boat to a complete stop, for had we done so, she would have been tossed around mercilessly at the will of the wind and seas, which would have made things even worse.

I proceeded by engaging the autopilot mode, meaning I would not have to stay there and steer the vessel as the autopilot would guide her for now in the rough seas. This maneuver allowed me to leave the helm, run downstairs and check out the situation. When I reached the hatch on the starboard side, which was now already wide open, I climbed down the stairs unhindered and into the depths of the pontoon. What I saw next almost paralyzed my entire body because it was almost indescribable. As if I had just seen a monster standing in front of me, who would swallow me up.

I took a big breath as I struggled with my thoughts, trying to figure out what was happening and what I should do about this. I gasped for a deep breath of air, thinking that it might jar my brain for a quicker answer, as I walked within the pontoon with water high to my ankles and still rushing in. Again, I came to witness a very terrible sight, which nobody would want to see in their own boat.

The view of turquoise blue waters rushing into the hull, through where once upon a time there were bolts and nuts holding the fresh raw water seacock in place. But now, all this hardware was gone, all four nuts and bolts. I was only slightly relieved because it could have been worse, in that the entire seacock could have unhinged from the floor of the pontoon, but for now remained put. Had the seacock let loose, the amount of water would have been a million times worse, and we surely would have sunk within minutes. At least the holes where each bolt was missing were only a quarter of an inch wide, not as bad as had the seacock disconnected, whereupon the hole would have been approximately two inches. So in essence, the disappearance of the four bolts was approximately half the width of what the seacock hole would have been had it disconnected. In retrospect, the chances were in our favor for survival when one would weigh the possible outcome of four smaller holes, which could be closed off more easily than one large hole. But how would we even do that, close the four holes that I was looking at?

The water coming in was still voluminous and accumulated in the engine room beyond what the bilge pump could handle. Assessing the situation, I knew we had a problem, which we were not prepared for, but had a small amount of time to deal with it. At least we had some time to decide how to handle this. Not a lot of time, but some time. All in all, we did have an emergency, and we needed to handle it in a reasonable timeframe; otherwise, we would eventually sink. Our boat was too large to navigate through the Jupiter Inlet, so that route wasn't an option. Even if we had access to an inlet wide and deep enough for the Sea Scape, moving a vessel that size would require prior scheduling. In Florida, there are maybe two or three marinas that could do that, and they are few and far between. So, we were in a dire situation.

The water was rushing in, and I could see the depth of the turquoise blue ocean through the holes of the seacock, and that was scary. On the inner side of the pontoon closest to the midline, the four bolts holding the seacock to the fiberglass hull were no longer present. How did this happen? How did the four bolts disappear? But this was not the time to try to find the answer. We had an emergency at hand, and we had to act and react. All we knew was that they were no longer there.

Even though each of these holes was relatively small, only a quarter of an inch wide, the problem was imminent. The bilge pump was working but could not keep up with the amount of water entering. I must have looked extremely pale, and the only thought going through my mind was dealing with this emergency; otherwise, our boat would sink. Even in extreme fear, I tried to appeal to my logical and calm senses to come up with a plan. I rushed up the steps, out of the engine room towards the pilot house to hail the Coast Guard, Boat US and Sea Tow for our rescue. The boat was almost in line with the Jupiter Inlet now. We hoped—and quietly prayed—that being close to the inlet would help rescuers find us faster than if we'd been farther from a navigable entry point for rescue boats. It was a very uncomfortable feeling, to say the least. Thanks to our prayers, about twenty minutes later we saw the first signs of rescue vessels. As the Coast Guard vessel came close, they threw their fenders between our boat and theirs. Then one of their captains jumped onto our boat's platform at the stern. I asked them while they were on their way whether they had crash pumps with them, and they assured me that they did.

The Coast Guard captain climbed into the pontoon through the ladder, assessed the situation and, like us, knew that we needed to plug these holes. As if by a miracle, he and my mate found some metal wood screws and together shoved them into the holes. The water stopped gushing in. Success, success, hurrah, hurrah! We thanked them for helping us out, and they were on their way. We knew that this was a temporary solution, and we headed back to Fort Lauderdale to have a permanent repair done.

What I learned from that boating emergency was the following. Number one, crash pumps, which can pump out and remove a few hundred gallons a minute, are very important and necessary to have on a boat. But they require a 12V outlet. We happened to have the 12V outlets because we use electric reels when fishing. They are not expensive and can be wired and placed on any boat. Number two, we should have had an assortment of either wooden or synthetic plugs of various sizes on the boat, which we did not have. Number three, knowing the phone numbers and who to call is extremely important. Thank God we had a good VHF and good cell phone reception, which is what really saved us this time. Number four, we should have performed previous drills in preparation for any emergencies, which we had not previously done. The steps of recognition in an emergency, assessment and thoughts would have better prepared us to meet the challenges that these emergencies require.

To my amazement, it worked. The metal wood screws stopped the entry of water. But in truth, we were not prepared for such an emergency. We should have been better prepared. We should have had an assortment of pegs of different sizes and materials. But we did not. Also, we did not have crash pumps on board, which we should have had.

Where did the bolts and nuts disappear to? Were we having a problem with hydrolysis on the boat? We had that checked out, but there was no sign of that. Was it sabotage because the engine hatches are never locked? What exactly happened, we never found out. Every couple of weeks now, we do a detailed inspection of all our seacocks, trying to understand what happened. Experience is what you get when you don't get what you want, and that taught us a very important lesson. An emergency is an emergency, big or small. You learn so much from each other's experience in hopes of not repeating the same mistakes and learning how to handle them should they come. Reaction time and response can make all the difference between life and death, between staying afloat or sinking. Maybe by reading this book and sharing our experiences, we can stay connected to boating emergencies and how to handle them. Reaction times could become quicker when we are exposed to the possibilities of how and what could possibly happen. None of us wants to be caught "OFF GUARD."

Another short story that I would like to share about a boating emergency occurred about 20 miles offshore from Key West. Many years ago, I owned a 20-foot Grady White. My friend and I decided to fish, and after checking the forecast, it appeared that it would be a very nice day to go out. I had recently had new scuppers placed at the transom of my boat because the old ones were worn, and I noted that they were not holding the water back from flowing into the stern. Like everybody else, I like keeping my feet dry when on the boat, and I did not want to take on any additional water, which could eventuate in a problem while out in the ocean.

I therefore had the scuppers on both sides of the boat replaced with new ones. What I did not realize at the time they were changed is that they used ping-pong balls. Scuppers are drains on the deck or sides of a boat designed to let water out. A ping-pong ball placed within the scupper acts as a one-way valve. Under normal conditions, the ball sits loosely, allowing rainwater or deck wash to drain out easily. When the boat rolls, pitches, or takes on waves, incoming water pushes the ball upward against the opening, forming a temporary seal. The lightweight, buoyant ping-pong ball floats up immediately when water attempts to enter from outside, blocking the opening quickly and effectively. However, they failed us when we were 20 miles offshore fishing that day.

As we sat there fishing and enjoying ourselves, it seemed almost miraculous how quickly seawater began flooding the boat—within minutes, cushions and coolers were afloat. We were now a long way from land. At an initial glance, I could not determine exactly where within the boat this water was coming in from. I searched for a clue when I realized that the scuppers had given way. It appeared that these ping-pong balls became logged in such a manner that they allowed water from the outside ocean to come in but did not allow the water to drain out of the boat like a one-way valve.

As I lifted the fiberglass cover off the top of the transom in order to see how much water was inside the hull, I almost had a heart attack. The entire hull underneath was filled with saltwater, including the only two batteries we had on the boat, which were now covered by at least six inches of water above them. Oh my God! I really thought this was it, my end. I am speaking about the end of my life and my friend's life. As I turned pale white and almost lost control of all my senses, I began to silently pray to the Lord. Thoughts were jarring my mind. I made my way to the cockpit and, in a futile attempt, turned the ignition key—fully expecting silence, especially with both batteries submerged in seawater. Then, almost miraculously—and to my utter relief—the Yamaha engine roared back to life after a few seconds of eerie silence. I was thrilled, as was my friend. Without a moment's hesitation, I slammed the throttle forward—expecting us to surge toward home—but though the engine roared, the boat remained motionless. Oh my God, engine roaring or not, I thought we were dead because the boat did not make any headway. I waited and waited, hoping my luck again would change and suddenly, as hope eluded me for a little while, the engine's roar picked up and the boat started moving ever so slightly forward. "Oh my God," I humbly whispered, not to alarm my friend. He was already scared to death, as I was, and thought his life would also be over soon. However, again our prayers were answered. The boat began to move, but I could not get it on plane for a while. Minutes in my mind seemed like hours while waiting to plane the boat. But the boat was very heavy and filled with ocean water. Finally, after a few more minutes, the water must have gradually drained—perhaps as the ping-pong balls in the gunnel leading to the scupper came loose—allowing the water to escape and the boat to get up on plane.

We eventually made it home, where I had to have every electrical wire replaced in order to avoid corrosion. What I had learned from that experience was threefold. The first was that I should not have wandered off as far as I did with a small boat and with only one engine. Secondly, I should not have allowed the marina mechanics to put in this new invention of ping-pong balls before I tried using the boat in a more local surrounding. Lastly, if the same happened again, I later learned that had I jumped into the water to remove the drain plug on the lower edge of the transom, it would have allowed the water to drain a lot faster and more efficiently. Removing the drain plug would have been the answer as long as we could start the engine and get under way.

We all have stories that we could share with each other that have happened to each one of us. Each story is unique and tells a tale of its own. We usually share these stories with people closest to us, communicating the tales in the hope that our experiences will become documented, and lessons learned in order to learn from each experience. Boaters share a similar love for the waters in many ways and feel kinship with each other. If we all appreciate this and if we know how important it is to share boating emergency information, then some of these stories could be lifesaving. These failures and their triumphs should be passed from one generation to the next, in order to teach us the lesson that we must learn and get smarter. It's like lessons of history in many cultures that were not even written down but passed from one generation to the next.

One key takeaway I've learned—and strongly encourage— is that when navigating unfamiliar waters, even with the most advanced and up-to-date instruments, it's best practice to contact the nearest BoatUS or Sea Tow for local guidance.

There are many scenarios for boating emergencies. Many times when boating emergencies occur, they happen way offshore. So far that it may be hard to locate the help that is needed. This is one of the reasons that it is very important to rely on one's own knowledge and skill. That is one of the other reasons that this reference book may become handy. In my daily life, being a surgeon, I have often found variations in human anatomy. Even though I have an additional degree in human anatomy, I try to anticipate things that could come up unexpectedly. I need to prepare and be ready for any unexpected variations and situations that could arise. We all need to prepare and anticipate the same. Readiness, preparedness, anticipation, spare parts, tools and the will to survive, however hard it may be,, are very important in a dangerous situation.

This book aims to prepare you for almost any type of boating emergency and help you think through it so that the outcome will be successful. Give yourselves the opportunity to read this very important resource, scan through it and study the chapters, especially those you're least familiar with. At least when you encounter your boating emergency, you may feel a lot more confident and prepared, having taken the time to become familiar with what could go wrong. I pray for you and hope that the outcome of any emergency is successful. May God bless and protect you, but there is also another saying: God helps those who help themselves. Good luck with everything.

PART ONE

AN INTRODUCTION TO BOATING EMERGENCIES

CHAPTER 1

THE ANATOMY OF A BOAT'S RUNNING GEAR

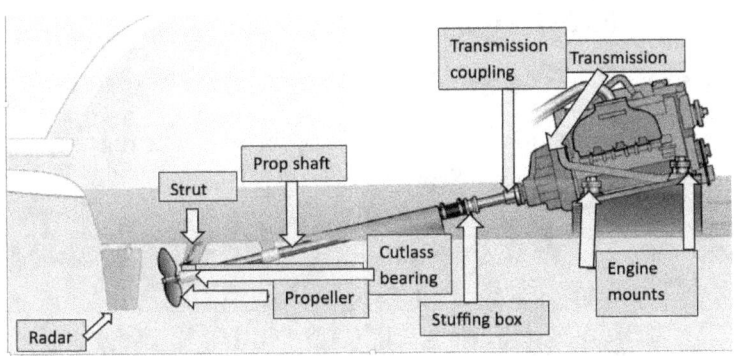

Key components of a marine propulsion system

Engine to Propeller Anatomy

Engine

- Generates propulsion power
- Inboard, outboard, or stern drive
- Components: Crankshaft, exhaust manifold, cooling system

Transmission (Gearbox)

- Transmits engine power, controls speed/direction
- Components: Input shaft, gears, output shaft

Coupling

- Connects transmission to propeller shaft, absorbs vibrations
- Rigid coupling, flexible coupling

Propeller Shaft

- Transfers energy from transmission to propeller
- Stainless steel, supported by bearings

Bearings

- Support shaft, smooth rotation
- Cutlass bearings, thrust bearings

Stern Tube

- Encases shaft exiting hull, prevents water ingress
- Components: Stuffing box, dripless seal

Strut

- Additional propeller shaft support
- Bronze/stainless steel, houses cutlass bearing

Propeller

- Converts shaft rotation into thrust
- Blades, pitch, stainless steel/bronze

Rudder (Optional but Related)

- Steers boat by directing water flow

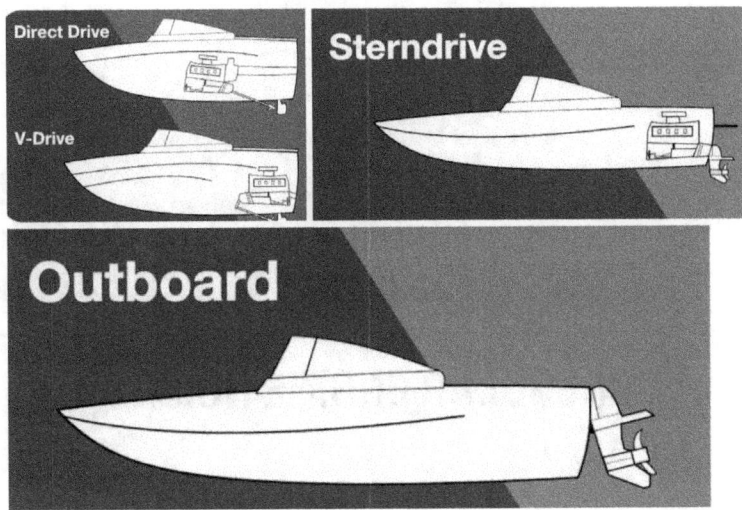

Common boat propulsion systems

Inspection Priority (High to Low Risk)

- Propeller damage/imbalance (High)
- Drivetrain misalignment (High)
- Damaged/worn engine mounts (High)
- Propeller fouling (Medium)
- Waterlogged hull/structural damage (Medium)
- Worn/damaged cutlass bearings (Medium)
- Loose/missing fasteners (Medium)
- Cavitation/aeration (Low)
- Overloaded/unbalanced boat (Low)
- Environmental factors (Low)

CHAPTER 2

IRREGULAR ENGINE NOISES

Knocking Sounds

Cause: Pre-Ignition or Detonation

- Pre-ignition occurs when fuel ignites prematurely, causing knocking
- Detonation is uncontrolled combustion due to excessive heat or pressure

Possible Culprits:

- Using fuel with lower octane rating
- Carbon buildup in combustion chamber
- Incorrect ignition timing
- Faulty spark plug

Sputtering or Stuttering

Cause: Fuel Delivery Issues

- Consistent clean fuel supply essential for smooth performance

Possible Culprits:

- Clogged fuel filters
- Air in fuel lines
- Dirty or faulty injectors
- Water or contaminants in fuel

Unusual Vibrations

Cause: Mechanical Imbalance

- Indicates mechanical issues

Possible Culprits:

- Misaligned or bent propeller shaft
- Damaged/unbalanced propeller blades
- Loose or worn engine mounts
- Uneven cylinder compression

Whining or Whistling Sounds

Cause: Airflow or Belt Issues

- Unusual airflow or worn components create high-pitched noises

Possible Culprits:

- Worn/loose alternator or water pump belts
- Air leaks in intake manifold or throttle body
- Obstructed air filters

Pinging or Ticking

Cause: Valve or Exhaust System Issues

- Small ticking sounds from valve components or exhaust leaks

Possible Culprits:

- Incorrect valve clearance
- Worn or loose rocker arms/lifters
- Exhaust manifold leaks

Low Rumbling or Roaring

Cause: Exhaust System Issues

- Exhaust critical for noise and emissions control

Possible Culprits:

- Exhaust leaks or broken mufflers
- Damaged or missing muffler baffles

Chugging or Misfiring

Cause: Ignition Problems

- Proper ignition timing ensures smooth combustion

Possible Culprits:

- Worn or damaged spark plugs
- Faulty ignition coils or wires
- Moisture or corrosion in ignition system

Chapter 3

BOAT VIBRATIONS

HIGH RISK VIBRATIONS

Propeller Damage or Imbalance
- A bent, chipped, or fouled propeller can severely damage the drivetrain.
- Inspect blades for cracks, bends, or missing sections.
- Check for marine growth or entangled debris.
- Examine shaft for alignment issues and physical damage.
- Ensure propeller is securely mounted.
- Clean, repair, or replace propeller; realign shaft if bent.

Drivetrain Misalignment
- Engine or shaft misalignment causes vibrations and risks transmission damage.
- Use a feeler gauge to check coupling gaps.
- Inspect cutlass bearings for play or wear.
- Look for worn rubber or loose bolts in couplings.
- Realign drivetrain; replace damaged bearings or couplings.

Damaged or Worn Engine Mounts

- Failing mounts allow engine movement and stress components.
- Check bolts for tightness and proper torque.
- Inspect rubber mounts for cracks or deformation.
- Observe engine during operation for excessive motion.
- Tighten or replace mounts as necessary.

MEDIUM RISK VIBRATIONS

Propeller Fouling

- Debris like lines or seaweed can imbalance the propeller.
- Check blades and shaft for entanglement.
- Inspect intake grates for blockage.
- Manually remove debris or install a line cutter.

Waterlogged Hull or Structural Damage

- Excess water or hull deformities can cause instability.
- Inspect bilge for water buildup and proper drainage.
- Look for hull cracks, delamination, or damage.
- Pump water and repair hull if needed.

Worn or Damaged Cutlass Bearings

- Worn bearings cause shaft play and vibration.
- Check bearings for looseness around the shaft.
- Test for lateral shaft movement.
- Replace worn bearings immediately.

Loose or Missing Fasteners

- Loose bolts or nuts on drivetrain components can induce vibration.
- Inspect and tighten engine, transmission, and propeller hardware.

- Replace missing or corroded fasteners.

LOW RISK VIBRATIONS

Cavitation or Aeration Issues

- Air bubbles around the propeller cause vibration and inefficiency.
- Ensure the propeller is correctly matched to the boat/engine.
- Check for hull obstructions affecting water flow.
- Adjust propeller design or hull shape accordingly.

Overloaded or Unbalanced Boat

- Uneven loads increase drag and vibration.
- Confirm proper distribution of passengers and gear.
- Make sure total load is within the boat's capacity.
- Adjust and reduce load where needed.

Environmental Factors

- External conditions (waves, currents) may mimic vibration.
- Monitor wave conditions during travel.
- Adjust trim and speed to minimize external vibration.

Inspection Order Summary

Inspection Area	Risk Level
Propeller Damage or Imbalance	High
Drivetrain Misalignment	High
Damaged or Worn Engine Mounts	High

Inspection Area	Risk Level
Propeller Fouling	Medium
Waterlogged Hull or Structural Damage	Medium
Worn or Damaged Cutlass Bearings	Medium
Loose or Missing Fasteners	Medium
Cavitation or Aeration Issues	Low
Overloaded or Unbalanced Boat	Low
Environmental Factors	Low

Preventive Measures

- Conduct regular inspections of propeller, shaft, engine mounts, and drivetrain.
- Replace worn bearings, couplings, or mounts before failure.
- Maintain even weight distribution; avoid exceeding boat's load limits.
- Avoid areas with heavy debris or shallow waters to prevent propeller fouling.

Chapter 4

IRREGULAR POWER OUTPUT

Fuel Delivery Issues

- Contaminated fuel
- Clogged fuel filters
- Fuel pump malfunction
- Faulty fuel injectors

Sudden Power Loss in a Marine Engine

- **Fuel System Issues:** Starvation, contamination, faulty pump
- **Electrical System Failures:** Weak battery, faulty ignition, alternator failure
- **Cooling System Problems:** Overheating, blocked cooling
- **Propulsion Issues:** Fouled or damaged propeller
- **Airflow Restrictions:** Clogged air filter
- **Mechanical Failures:** Low oil pressure, internal engine issues

- **Exhaust Blockages:** Blocked exhaust outlet
- **Sensor/Computer Failures:** Faulty sensors or ECU malfunction
- **Environmental Factors:** Water ingress, extreme weather

Preventive Measures

- Conduct regular inspections
- Perform routine maintenance
- Ensure proper weight distribution
- Avoid debris-filled waters

CHAPTER 5

ADRIFT IN STRONG CURRENTS AND BUSY WATERWAYS

Drifting and Loss of Control

Strong Currents

- The boat may drift uncontrollably towards obstacles or hazardous zones
- Increased risk of grounding, collisions, or capsizing
- Deploy anchor immediately to stabilize and prevent drifting
- If anchoring impossible, use paddles, oars, or trolling motor to maintain control

Busy Waterways

- Loss of control in high-traffic areas, increasing collision risk
- Danger to passengers, vessel damage, potential liability
- Signal nearby boats with distress signals (flares, lights, flags)
- Use horn or whistle to communicate clearly to surrounding vessels

Collision Risks

Stationary Objects

- Drifting into rocks, docks, bridges, or buoys, causing damage
- Potential hull breaches or capsizing
- Identify obstacles and manually navigate away with paddles or steering
- Call for assistance if control can't be regained

Moving Vessels

- Risk of being struck by passing boats
- Life-threatening collisions and damage to vessels
- Use visual and audible signals to increase visibility and warn others

Passenger Safety

Panic and Injury

- Passengers panicking or moving unpredictably, increasing onboard accidents
- Potential injuries or falls overboard
- Keep passengers calm, seated, wearing life jackets
- Assign passenger roles (deploying anchor, signaling for help)

Overboard Risks

- Passengers falling overboard in currents, risk of being swept away
- Difficulty retrieving overboard individuals
- Conduct headcount; ensure everyone onboard is accounted for

- Use throwable flotation devices to assist those overboard

Environmental Hazards

Weather Conditions

- Strong winds, waves, storms worsen drift and increase capsizing risk
- Secure loose items onboard
- Deploy drogue or sea anchor to stabilize boat and reduce drift speed

Tides and Shallow Waters

- Risk of being pushed into shallow waters or reefs causing damage
- Monitor depth readings, avoid shallow areas

Communication Challenges

Lack of Visibility

- Poor visibility delays rescue efforts
- Activate visual distress signals (flares, strobe lights, reflective gear)

No Radio Contact

- Communication system failure leaves you unable to call for help
- Use handheld VHF or satellite phone if available
- Use visual or sound signals if communication devices fail

Potential Emergency Situations

Engine Repairs in Dangerous Conditions

- Risk of crew injury or boat damage attempting repairs
- Prioritize safety; attempt repairs only in stable conditions

Running Out of Resources

- Extended time adrift risks running out of food, water, safety gear
- Ration supplies, keep passengers hydrated and sheltered
- Use survival gear (blankets, tarps) for protection

Legal and Environmental Considerations

Environmental Damage

- Fuel or oil spills harming marine life
- Contain spills using absorbent materials; report incidents

Legal Liability

- Collisions or damages caused by drifting could result in liability
- Document events; communicate with authorities or insurance promptly

Emergency Actions Summary

- Deploy anchor immediately in currents
- Signal nearby vessels in busy waterways
- Keep passengers seated and calm with life jackets

- Secure loose items and monitor environmental conditions
- Utilize all available communication tools for distress signaling
- Prioritize passenger safety and stable conditions before engine repair
- Monitor depth and environmental risks; contain leaks or spills promptly

Conclusion

In strong currents or busy waterways, promptly stabilizing the vessel, signaling for assistance, and ensuring passenger safety are top priorities. Proper preparation and regular maintenance reduce the likelihood and severity of such emergencies.

Chapter 6

DEALING WITH LIMITED MANEUVERABILITY

Immediate Steps to Regain Control

Deploy the Anchor

- Purpose: Stabilize the boat, prevent uncontrolled drifting
- Drop anchor immediately; deploy sufficient anchor line (scope of 7:1)

Assess the Situation

- Purpose: Identify hazards, determine best actions
- Check for obstacles, vessels, shallow waters
- Evaluate current and wind direction

Use Alternative Maneuvering Techniques

Use Paddles or Oars

- Purpose: Provide basic propulsion and directional control

- Assign crew to paddle on opposite sides, coordinate movements

Deploy a Trolling Motor

- Purpose: Low-speed propulsion in calm conditions
- Use trolling motor to steer toward safe location

Adjust Trim and Balance

- Purpose: Improve handling, reduce resistance
- Shift weight evenly, adjust trim tabs or outdrive

Signal for Assistance

Visual Signals

- Purpose: Alert nearby vessels
- Use distress flags, flares, reflective mirrors, orange "V" signal flag

Audible Signals

- Purpose: Warn vessels of limited maneuverability
- Sound horn in series of long blasts, use whistle if horn unavailable

VHF Radio Communication

- Purpose: Call for assistance, inform nearby vessels
- Broadcast position, situation, request for help (Channel 114)
- Example: "Mayday, this is [Boat Name], currently adrift near [location], require immediate assistance due to engine failure."

Maneuvering Using Environmental Factors

Utilize Wind

- Purpose: Steer or drift boat toward safety
- Use paddle or rudder to adjust boat angle, deploy sail if available

Work with Currents

- Purpose: Move boat with water flow
- Steer toward calmer areas, avoid hazardous strong currents

Plan Navigation and Safety

Avoid Hazards

- Purpose: Prevent collisions or grounding
- Identify and avoid rocks, reefs, docks, vessels using charts/GPS

Direct the Boat to a Safe Area

- Purpose: Ensure passenger and vessel safety
- Steer toward nearest calm water, dock, or anchoring point

Passenger and Crew Safety

Distribute Life Jackets

- Purpose: Prepare everyone onboard for emergencies
- Passengers wear life jackets, brief on evacuation plans

Assign Roles

- Purpose: Organize tasks efficiently
- Designate crew to anchor deployment, paddling, signaling

- Assign someone to monitor surroundings and handle communication

If Drifting in a Busy Waterway

Increase Visibility
- Purpose: Alert other vessels of limited maneuverability
- Use flashing lights, reflective materials, flares
- Position crew with bright flags or clothing

Maintain Communication
- Purpose: Inform other vessels clearly
- Use VHF radio or sound signals, maintain continuous communication

Preventive Measures

Regular Maintenance
- Purpose: Reduce power loss likelihood
- Routine checks of engine, fuel system, electrical components

Carry Backup Systems
- Purpose: Alternative propulsion or power
- Carry charged trolling motor, extra paddles, spare batteries

Pre-Trip Preparation
- Purpose: Ensure readiness for emergencies
- Inspect safety gear, test engine, review weather conditions

Summary of Actions

- Stabilize boat: Deploy anchor and assess surroundings
- Alternative propulsion: Use paddles, trolling motor, adjust trim
- Signal for help: Use VHF radio, flares, audible signals
- Utilize environment: Steer using wind and currents
- Prioritize safety: Life jackets, assign crew tasks, passenger calmness
- Avoid hazards: Manual steering clear of obstacles, busy areas

Conclusion

Quick thinking, resourcefulness, and maintaining calm are key to safely handling limited maneuverability. Stabilizing the boat, using alternative methods of propulsion, and clearly signaling for assistance significantly reduce risks. Proper preparation and routine maintenance help prevent these emergencies.

PART TWO

PREVENTION IS KEY

CHAPTER 7

VESSEL INSPECTION CHECKLIST

Structural Integrity

- Check the hull for cracks, dents, or signs of wear.
- Inspect the deck for stability and secure fittings.
- Ensure railings and lifelines are firmly attached.
- Check seals and latches on windows and hatches for watertight integrity.

Engine and Mechanical Systems

- Verify fuel levels and inspect tanks for leaks or corrosion.
- Check fuel lines for cracks, kinks, or loose fittings.
- Inspect engine oil and coolant levels; check for leaks.
- Examine belts for tension and wear.
- Check hoses for cracks, bulges, or leaks.
- Ensure batteries are fully charged and securely mounted.
- Check battery connections for corrosion and clean if needed.

- Inspect the propeller for damage and ensure the shaft rotates smoothly.

Electrical Systems

- Test all navigation lights and replace any burnt-out bulbs.
- Verify VHF radio functionality and backup communication devices.
- Check that all instrument panel gauges are operational.
- Test EPIRBs or PLBs for proper function.
- Ensure circuit breakers are reset and fuses are intact.

Safety Equipment

- Ensure a properly sized, U.S. Coast Guard-approved life jacket for each passenger.
- Inspect life jackets for damage, tears, or mold.
- Confirm the presence and charge of required fire extinguishers.
- Check flares and signaling devices for expiration dates and functionality.
- Include a backup whistle, mirror, and flashlight.
- Confirm that the first aid kit is complete and stocked.
- Check that throwable flotation devices are accessible.
- Inspect the anchor for integrity and ensure the line is in good condition.

Navigation and Steering

- Ensure up-to-date nautical charts are onboard.
- Test GPS and backup navigation tools.
- Verify the compass is properly calibrated and functional.

- Check for smooth operation of the steering system.
- Inspect hydraulic or cable connections for wear or leaks.

Plumbing and Bilge Systems

- Test automatic and manual bilge pumps for functionality.
- Ensure backup pumps are available and operational.
- Check water tanks for leaks and sufficient potable water levels.
- Inspect marine toilets and ensure holding tanks are empty and sealed properly.

Fueling and Ventilation

- Ensure fuel tanks are full and free of water or debris.
- Test bilge blowers to confirm proper ventilation of fuel vapors before starting the engine.

Emergency and Backup Systems

- Carry spare parts, including fuses, belts, filters, spark plugs, and propellers.
- Stock a basic tool kit for onboard repairs.
- Include food, water, and thermal blankets for emergencies.
- Ensure portable power sources (e.g., generators, solar chargers) are operational.

Environmental and Weather Preparation

- Check marine weather forecasts before departure.
- Review tide tables and understand current patterns.

- File a float plan with someone onshore, including itinerary and expected return time.

Communication and Documentation

- Ensure vessel registration and operator licenses are onboard and up to date.
- Carry copies of insurance documentation.
- Have a list of emergency contacts, including the Coast Guard and local rescue services.

Chapter 8

SAFETY GEAR AND EQUIPMENT

Personal Safety Equipment

- One U.S. Coast Guard-approved life jacket per person, appropriately sized.
- Inspect PFDs for wear, buoyancy, and secure straps.
- Ensure PFDs are easily accessible.
- Have throwable flotation devices (e.g., ring buoys, cushions with handles).
- Ensure compliance with regulations for throwable devices on boats over 114 feet.
- Carry survival suits for cold water environments.
- Inspect harnesses and tethers for secure attachment points and wear.

Fire Safety Equipment

- Ensure fire extinguishers are ABC- or BC-rated and properly placed.
- Verify fire extinguishers are fully charged and within their expiration date.
- Test smoke detectors and replace batteries as needed.

- Have fire blankets available for smothering small fires.

Navigation and Communication Tools

- Test VHF marine radios, including a backup handheld radio.
- Ensure EPIRBs (automatic and manual) are functional.
- Check expiration dates and accessibility of flares and signaling devices.
- Carry whistles and horns for audible emergency signals.
- Test all navigation lights before departure.

Emergency Kits

- Stock a first aid kit with bandages, antiseptics, medications, and burn treatments.
- Regularly inspect and replenish the first aid kit.
- Pack a survival kit with flashlights, emergency blankets, water filters, and food.
- Carry a tool kit with wrenches, screwdrivers, duct tape, and spare fuses.

Anchoring and Mooring Equipment

- Have appropriate anchors (Danforth, plow, or mushroom) based on water conditions.
- Inspect anchor line and chain for wear.
- Check mooring lines for fraying or weakness.

Bilge and Flooding Equipment

- Test automatic and manual bilge pumps regularly.
- Carry backup bilge pumps.

- Have buckets available for manual water removal.

Environmental Safety Equipment

- Ensure life rafts are properly inflated and stocked with survival gear.
- Have drift anchors to stabilize the vessel in rough seas.
- Pack sun protection gear (sunscreen, hats, UV-protective clothing).

Backup Power Sources

- Carry spare batteries for radios and navigation tools.
- Ensure portable generators are operational.

Regulatory Compliance

- Keep vessel registration, licenses, and insurance onboard.
- Verify proof of compliance with local safety regulations.
- Ensure valid Coast Guard or local authority inspection stickers.

Training and Familiarity

- Conduct regular safety drills for emergencies (fire, man overboard, etc.).
- Demonstrate the use of safety gear to all passengers.
- Assign roles and responsibilities for emergency situations.

Conclusion

- Regularly inspect, maintain, and familiarize all passengers with safety equipment.
- Prioritize safety before every trip to ensure preparedness for emergencies.

CHAPTER 9

FUEL AND ENGINE CHECKS

Fuel System Checks

- Check fuel levels before departure, ensuring a sufficient reserve.
- Follow the "Rule of Thirds" for fuel allocation.
- Ensure portable fuel tanks are full and securely connected.
- Inspect fuel for contamination (water, debris, microbial growth).
- Use fuel stabilizers to maintain fuel quality.
- Inspect fuel lines for leaks, cracks, or corrosion.
- Perform a flex test on fuel hoses to check for brittleness.
- Ensure all fuel clamps and connections are secure.
- Clear fuel tank vents of debris for proper airflow.
- Use bilge blowers before starting the engine to remove fuel vapors.
- Carry spare fuel in approved containers, stored safely.

Engine Checks

- Check engine oil levels using the dipstick.

- Inspect oil for discoloration or debris.
- Follow manufacturer's oil change schedule.
- Ensure coolant reservoir is full and free of leaks.
- Inspect cooling system hoses for cracks or wear.
- Flush the coolant system periodically to prevent overheating.
- Check drive belts for fraying, cracks, or wear.
- Ensure proper belt tension to prevent slipping or strain.
- Inspect cooling and fuel hoses for blockages or damage.
- Test the battery charge level before departure.
- Clean and tighten battery terminals.
- Carry a backup battery or portable jump starter.
- Inspect propeller for damage (bent or chipped blades).
- Ensure the propeller shaft rotates freely and is securely fastened.

Maintenance Practices

- Schedule professional servicing as per manufacturer's guidelines.
- Maintain a detailed maintenance and repair log.
- Keep essential spare parts onboard (belts, spark plugs, filters, fuel line connectors).
- Carry a tool kit with wrenches, screwdrivers, pliers, and duct tape.
- Winterize the engine before extended cold-weather storage.
- De-winterize the engine and fuel system before the boating season.

Troubleshooting Common Engine Issues

- **If the engine won't start:** Check battery, fuel supply, and ignition system.

- **If the engine overheats:** Refill coolant, clear water intake, inspect impeller.
- **If the boat loses power:** Check for fuel contamination, clogged filters, or propeller damage.

Emergency Preparedness

- Install an engine monitoring system to detect issues early.
- Ensure VHF radios or satellite phones are operational.
- Carry a portable generator or backup power source.

Conclusion

- Conduct thorough fuel and engine checks before every trip.
- Follow regular maintenance schedules to prevent breakdowns.
- Stay prepared with troubleshooting knowledge and backup systems.

CHAPTER 10

WEATHER MONITORING

Importance of Weather Monitoring

- Monitor weather conditions to detect and avoid hazardous situations.
- Plan routes and departure times based on weather forecasts.
- Be prepared to delay or cancel trips due to severe weather warnings.
- Protect lives and property by staying informed of weather risks.

Tools for Weather Monitoring

- Check NOAA Marine Weather Forecasts, local meteorological agencies, or weather apps.
- Monitor VHF radio weather channels for real-time updates and emergency alerts.
- Use a barometer to track atmospheric pressure changes for storm predictions.
- Utilize radar systems for detecting approaching storms, especially offshore.

- Subscribe to satellite weather services for real-time updates in remote areas.

Weather Signs to Monitor

- Watch for dark, towering clouds (cumulonimbus) that indicate storms.
- Observe water surface conditions for choppy waves and erratic patterns.
- Pay attention to sudden wind gusts or changes in direction.
- Be alert to sudden temperature drops and increased humidity levels.

Planning Based on Weather Conditions

- Check forecasts for departure, route, and destination before boating.
- Avoid travel during gale warnings, high wind advisories, or thunderstorms.
- Plan routes that provide safe harbors or shelter from rough weather.
- Schedule departures during calm weather windows.

Responding to Sudden Weather Changes

- Reduce speed to maintain control and minimize wave impact.
- Seek shelter in a protected bay or behind natural barriers.
- Secure all loose equipment to prevent injuries and damage.
- Ensure all passengers are wearing life jackets.

- Activate radar, GPS, and navigation lights in low-visibility conditions.
- Communicate with nearby vessels or the Coast Guard via VHF radio

Special Weather Conditions to Watch

- **Thunderstorms** – Avoid open water, disconnect electronics, and seek shelter.
- **Fog** – Reduce speed, use foghorns, and navigate with radar and GPS.
- **Strong Currents & Tides** – Plan around slack tides and avoid strong flows.
- **Hurricanes & Tropical Storms** – Avoid boating in high-risk areas and heed evacuation warnings.

Technology and Advanced Weather Monitoring

- Use weather apps (e.g., Windy, PredictWind, Weather Underground) for real-time forecasts.
- Utilize AIS (Automatic Identification Systems) to track vessels and weather changes.
- Equip the boat with digital barometers and anemometers for accurate readings.

Key Takeaways for Weather Monitoring

- Always check weather forecasts before and during a trip.
- Equip the boat with reliable weather monitoring tools.
- Train passengers and crew on weather signs and emergency responses.

- Avoid boating in unfavorable or rapidly changing weather.

Conclusion

- Stay informed and vigilant to prevent emergencies caused by weather.
- Use technology and forecasting tools to enhance safety.
- Adjust plans as needed to ensure a safe boating experience.

CHAPTER 11

BOATER EDUCATION COURSES

Importance of Boater Education Courses

- Take a structured boating course to build confidence in vessel operation.
- Update knowledge on modern boating techniques, tools, and regulations.
- Reduce the risk of accidents by learning proper decision-making and safety protocols.
- Ensure compliance with legal requirements for boating licenses and regulations.

Core Topics Covered in Boater Education Courses

- Learn the basics of boat types, terminology, and maintenance.
- Understand navigation rules, including right-of-way and use of nautical charts.
- Gain knowledge of marine weather patterns and how to respond to severe conditions.

- Become familiar with essential safety equipment and proper emergency procedures.
- Receive first aid training for handling onboard medical emergencies.
- Learn environmental responsibilities, such as pollution prevention and marine conservation.
- Understand state and local boating laws, including speed limits and registration requirements.

Types of Boater Education Courses

- **Classroom-Based Courses** – Hands-on training and direct instructor interaction.
- **Online Courses** – Flexible, self-paced learning with quizzes and certification exams.
- **Practical Training Programs** – Real-world experience in docking, anchoring, and rough sea navigation.
- **Advanced Certification Programs** – Specialized training in offshore navigation and survival skills.

Benefits of Boater Education Courses

- Improve overall safety by learning best practices for emergency prevention.
- Enhance vessel handling, navigation, and emergency response skills.
- Reduce insurance costs by completing certified courses.
- Gain confidence and preparedness to handle unexpected situations effectively.

CHAPTER II

How to Choose the Right Course

- Verify that the course is accredited by NASBLA or the U.S. Coast Guard Auxiliary.
- Ensure the course covers essential topics like safety, navigation, and emergency response.
- Select a learning format that fits your schedule and preferred learning style.
- Confirm that the course provides a certification upon completion.

Additional Resources for Boater Education

- Download boating safety apps for real-time weather updates and navigation tools.
- Join local boating clubs for hands-on training sessions and practice drills.
- Participate in Coast Guard Auxiliary safety courses and vessel inspections.
- Explore online resources like BoatEd and U.S. Power Squadrons for additional training.

Key Takeaways

- Boater education is crucial for safety, reducing accidents, and improving boating skills.
- Certification from an accredited course may be required for licensing and insurance discounts.
- Choosing the right course ensures maximum benefits tailored to experience and needs.

Conclusion

- Commit to continuous learning to navigate safely and responsibly.
- Stay informed on best practices and regulations to prevent boating emergencies.
- Take advantage of educational resources to enhance boating knowledge and confidence.

CHAPTER 12

EMERGENCY DRILLS

A Vital Practice for Avoiding Boating Emergencies

Importance of Emergency Drills

- Familiarize passengers and crew with emergency protocols.
- Identify gaps in knowledge or equipment readiness before emergencies occur.
- Establish clear roles and responsibilities for each person onboard.
- Promote teamwork and minimize confusion during critical moments.
- Reduce panic by ensuring calm, controlled responses in emergencies.
- Ensure compliance with legal regulations for safety drills.

Types of Emergency Drills

Man Overboard (MOB) Drill

- Sound the alarm and assign a spotter.
- Throw a flotation device to the person in the water.
- Maneuver the boat to approach the MOB safely.
- Use rescue equipment to bring the person onboard.

Fire Drill

- Identify the fire location and sound the alarm.
- Use fire extinguishers and blankets to contain flames.
- Ensure all passengers wear life jackets.
- Review evacuation procedures if needed.

Abandon Ship Drill

- Sound the alarm and ensure all passengers wear life jackets.
- Gather at the muster station and deploy lifeboats.
- Practice using emergency signaling devices like flares and whistles.

Collision Drill

- Assess the damage and assign crew to manage leaks.
- Use bilge pumps to remove water if necessary.
- Prepare for evacuation if the vessel is at risk.

Medical Emergency Drill

- Practice administering first aid for common injuries.
- Simulate performing CPR on a dummy.
- Use onboard communication tools to call for medical help.

Severe Weather Drill

- Secure loose items and have passengers wear life jackets.

- Adjust speed and course for rough seas.
- Review the use of navigation and communication equipment.

How to Conduct Emergency Drills

Pre-Drill Preparation

- Develop a step-by-step emergency plan.
- Assign specific roles to passengers and crew.
- Provide a safety briefing before the drill.

Practice Scenarios

- Conduct drills in different conditions (day/night, calm/rough seas).
- Simulate real emergency situations for effective training.

Incorporate Equipment

- Ensure everyone knows the location and proper use of safety gear.
- Practice using life jackets, fire extinguishers, and emergency beacons.

Simulate Communication

- Practice making distress calls using a VHF radio.
- Use visual and audible signals to alert nearby vessels.

Review and Debrief

- Evaluate the effectiveness of the drill.
- Identify areas for improvement and update emergency procedures.

Frequency of Emergency Drills

- **Recreational Boaters:** At least one drill before each boating season or long trip.
- **Commercial Vessels:** Follow regulations requiring monthly or quarterly drills.
- **Long Voyages:** Conduct periodic drills to maintain preparedness.

Benefits of Emergency Drills

- Increase safety awareness among passengers and crew.
- Improve response times through repeated practice.
- Enhance teamwork and coordination during emergencies.
- Reduce liability by demonstrating proactive safety measures.

Challenges in Conducting Emergency Drills

- **Time Constraints:** Finding time amidst operational schedules.
- **Resistance from Participants:** Overcoming reluctance from crew and passengers.
- **Environmental Conditions:** Adapting drills for varying weather conditions.

Best Practices for Successful Drills

- Set a routine and integrate drills into regular boating practice.
- Engage all passengers and crew, regardless of experience level.

- Keep scenarios realistic to ensure serious participation.
- Encourage feedback to improve future drills.

Conclusion

- Commit to regular emergency drills to improve safety and preparedness.
- Familiarize everyone onboard with emergency procedures.
- Build confidence and coordination to handle unexpected situations effectively.

CHAPTER 13

READING NAUTICAL CHARTS

Understanding Nautical Charts

- Know that nautical charts provide essential navigation information.
- Familiarize yourself with key features, including water depths, hazards, and navigation aids.
- Understand symbols for buoys, beacons, shipwrecks, and contour lines.

Importance of Reading Nautical Charts

- Identify shallow areas, submerged objects, and hazards to avoid running aground.
- Use charts as a backup if GPS or electronic navigation systems fail.
- Locate protected harbors for shelter during storms.
- Plan refueling stops and supply points.
- Use charts for accurate location reporting in emergencies.
- Check tidal patterns and currents to navigate safely.

Key Elements of a Nautical Chart

- Understand depth contours to determine safe passages.
- Recognize buoys, beacons, and lighthouses for navigation assistance.
- Use the compass rose for accurate direction plotting.
- Interpret chart scale and symbols to understand details.
- Use latitude and longitude for precise location identification.
- Check tide and current tables for updated water movement data.

Using Navigational Charts During Emergencies

- Plot your position using a compass, landmarks, or known coordinates.
- Plan an alternate route if the original path is unsafe.
- Communicate clearly with rescuers, providing accurate coordinates and landmarks.
- Avoid additional hazards by steering clear of reefs, wrecks, and strong currents.

Best Practices for Using Nautical Charts

- Regularly update nautical charts to reflect current conditions.
- Review routes and potential hazards before setting sail.
- Use charts alongside GPS, radar, and depth finders for better accuracy.
- Practice reading and using charts during short trips.
- Keep paper charts onboard as a backup to electronic systems.

Training and Skill Development

- Take boater education courses that cover chart reading.
- Utilize online tutorials and interactive resources for practice.
- Conduct practical navigation drills using paper and digital charts.

By following this checklist, boaters can enhance their navigation skills, improve safety, and effectively respond to emergencies while on the water.

PART THREE

SAFETY CULTURE ON THE WATER

CHAPTER 14

ESTABLISHING ROLES AND RESPONSIBILITIES

Importance of Establishing Roles and Responsibilities

Promotes Order During Emergencies

- Clear roles prevent chaos and confusion when quick decisions are required.
- Ensures all necessary tasks are performed without duplication or oversight.

Enhances Team Coordination

- Roles streamline communication and allow individuals to focus on specific tasks.
- Encourages teamwork, where each person contributes to overall safety.

Increases Preparedness

- Assigning responsibilities ensures all safety equipment and procedures are understood before an emergency occurs.

Reduces Panic

- Knowing what to do fosters confidence, reducing fear or hesitation during emergencies.

Key Roles and Their Responsibilities

The Captain (Boat Operator)

Primary Responsibilities:

- Overall command of the vessel.
- Making critical decisions, including whether to abandon the boat.
- Navigating and steering the boat to safety.
- Ensuring all passengers are briefed on safety protocols.

In Emergencies:

- Communicate clearly with passengers and assign emergency roles.
- Coordinate with rescue services using VHF radio or signaling devices.

First Mate (Second-in-Command)

Primary Responsibilities:

- Assisting the captain in navigation and decision-making.
- Overseeing the readiness of safety equipment, including life jackets, fire extinguishers, and medical kits.

In Emergencies:

- Take over the captain's duties if they are incapacitated.
- Supervise evacuation procedures and assist with deploying life rafts or flotation devices.

Communications Officer

Primary Responsibilities:

- Handling all onboard communication equipment, such as VHF radios, EPIRBs, and satellite phones.
- Monitoring weather forecasts and emergency channels.

In Emergencies:

- Send distress signals and maintain contact with rescue services.
- Provide accurate updates on the vessel's location and situation.

Safety Officer

Primary Responsibilities:

- Conducting pre-departure safety briefings and equipment checks.
- Ensuring that safety gear is accessible and operational.

In Emergencies:

- Distribute life jackets and flotation devices.
- Direct passengers to muster points and manage onboard safety measures.

Rescue Coordinator

Primary Responsibilities:

- Organizing man overboard rescues or other retrieval operations.
- Deploying rescue equipment, such as throw bags or lifelines.

In Emergencies:

- Supervise the recovery of individuals in the water.
- Ensure proper use of rescue gear.

Medical Officer

Primary Responsibilities:

- Maintaining and organizing the first aid kit.
- Being knowledgeable about CPR and basic first aid procedures.

In Emergencies:

- Administer immediate care to injured or ill individuals.
- Assist with stabilizing patients until professional help arrives.

Passenger Roles

Responsibilities:

- Follow instructions from crew members or the captain.
- Familiarize themselves with safety protocols, including the location of life jackets and emergency exits.

In Emergencies:

- Assist with simple tasks if needed, such as securing equipment or helping others put on life jackets.

Preparing Roles Before a Trip

Pre-Departure Briefing

- Assign specific roles to individuals based on their skills,

experience, or physical ability.
- Conduct a safety briefing that includes:
- Location and use of safety equipment.
- Emergency procedures for common situations (e.g., fire, man overboard).

Role Practice

- Conduct emergency drills to ensure everyone understands their responsibilities.
- Rotate roles periodically so passengers and crew gain experience in multiple tasks.

Role Cards

- Provide laminated cards that outline specific responsibilities for each role.
- Include step-by-step instructions for tasks like operating the radio or deploying rescue equipment.

Challenges in Role Assignments

Lack of Experience

- Not all passengers or crew members may have boating experience.
- **Solution:** Provide basic training and assign less critical roles to inexperienced individuals.

Overlapping Duties

- Some emergencies may require one person to manage multiple tasks.
- **Solution:** Assign backups for critical roles to ensure continuity.

Resistance to Authority

- Passengers may hesitate to follow instructions in high-

stress situations.
- **Solution:** Emphasize the importance of following assigned roles during pre-departure briefings.

Adapting Roles During Emergencies

Reassigning Duties
- If a crew member is injured or incapacitated, their role should be reassigned promptly.
- Ensure backup personnel are prepared to step into critical roles.

Flexibility
- Be prepared to adjust roles based on the nature and severity of the emergency.
- Example: If multiple passengers fall overboard, prioritize rescue operations over communications.

Training and Resources

Boating Safety Courses
- Enroll crew members in certified courses that teach navigation, emergency management, and first aid.

Emergency Drills
- Practice realistic scenarios to test and refine assigned roles.

Written Emergency Plans
- Maintain a detailed plan outlining roles, responsibilities, and procedures for various emergencies.

Key Benefits of Defined Roles

Faster Response Times

- Clearly defined roles ensure tasks are completed quickly and efficiently.

Better Resource Management

- Proper coordination reduces duplication of effort and ensures resources are used effectively.

Increased Safety

- Roles help prevent panic and chaos, ensuring a calmer and more controlled response to emergencies.

Legal and Regulatory Compliance

- Demonstrating adherence to safety protocols can reduce liability in case of an accident.

Conclusion

- Establishing roles and responsibilities is a fundamental component of boating safety.
- By assigning tasks, providing training, and practicing drills, boaters can ensure that emergencies are handled efficiently and effectively.
- Whether on a recreational trip or a commercial voyage, clear roles enhance preparedness, protect lives, and promote a safer boating experience.

Chapter 15

ENCOURAGING A SAFETY-FIRST MINDSET, PREVENTION IS THE KEY

Encouraging a Safety-First Mindset to Prevent Boating Emergencies

- A safety-first mindset is fundamental for preventing boating emergencies and ensuring the well-being of everyone onboard.
- It involves fostering a culture where safety takes precedence over convenience or haste.
- By prioritizing proactive measures, educating passengers and crew, and reinforcing safe behaviors, boaters can significantly reduce the likelihood of accidents and improve responses during emergencies.

What is a Safety-First Mindset?

- A safety-first mindset refers to the consistent practice of prioritizing safety considerations in all boating activities. It includes:

- Anticipating potential risks and taking preventive measures.
- Encouraging awareness and accountability among all onboard.
- Emphasizing the importance of preparation, training, and equipment maintenance.

Why a Safety-First Mindset is Crucial in Boating

a. Reduces Risk of Accidents

- Encourages adherence to navigation rules and weather warnings.
- Ensures regular maintenance of the vessel and equipment.

b. Improves Emergency Responses

- Prepares passengers and crew to handle unexpected incidents confidently.
- Reduces panic and confusion during high-pressure situations.

c. Protects Lives and Property

- Minimizes the risk of injury or fatalities through proper use of safety equipment.
- Prevents costly damages to the vessel by avoiding dangerous situations.

d. Enhances Boating Enjoyment

- Promotes a secure and stress-free environment for everyone onboard

How to Foster a Safety-First Mindset

a. Education and Training

1. Safety Briefings:
- Conduct pre-departure briefings to inform passengers of onboard safety rules.
- Highlight the location and use of emergency equipment, such as life jackets, fire extinguishers, and radios.

2. Boating Safety Courses:
- Enroll in certified courses to learn about navigation, emergency procedures, and local regulations.
- Encourage crew members and frequent passengers to complete basic safety training.

b. Proactive Planning

1. Pre-Trip Inspections:
- Conduct thorough checks of the vessel's hull, engine, fuel systems, and safety equipment.

2. Weather Monitoring:
- Regularly review marine weather forecasts and adjust plans as necessary.

3. Float Plans:
- File a float plan with a trusted person onshore, detailing the route, destination, and expected return time.

c. Emphasizing the Use of Safety Equipment

1. **Life Jackets:**
    - Ensure all passengers wear properly fitted life jackets at all times.

2. **Fire Extinguishers:**
    - Verify that fire extinguishers are charged and accessible.

3. **Emergency Communication Tools:**
    - Train passengers on the use of VHF radios, EPIRBs, and signaling devices.

d. Reinforcing Accountability

1. **Role Assignments:**
    - Assign specific roles to crew and passengers to ensure responsibilities are clear.
    - Rotate roles during drills to build familiarity with multiple safety tasks.

2. **Lead by Example:**
    - The captain or boat operator should model safe behaviors, such as adhering to speed limits and avoiding alcohol while operating the vessel.

Encouraging Safe Behavior Onboard

a. Enforcing Rules

- Clearly communicate and enforce rules, such as no running on deck or no leaning overboard.
- Address violations immediately to maintain a culture of accountability.

b. Discouraging Risky Activities

- Avoid behaviors that compromise safety, such as overloading the vessel or navigating at high speeds in restricted areas.
- Encourage passengers to report unsafe practices or potential hazards.

c. Promoting Situational Awareness

- Encourage everyone onboard to remain vigilant for changes in weather, water conditions, or nearby vessels.
- Teach passengers how to recognize and respond to potential hazards.

Incorporating Safety Drills

Regular practice reinforces a safety-first mindset by preparing everyone for emergencies. Examples include:

Man Overboard Drills:

- Practice spotting and retrieving individuals who fall overboard.

Fire Drills:

- Simulate onboard fires and rehearse containment and evacuation procedures.

Abandon Ship Drills:

- Practice donning life jackets, deploying life rafts, and using signaling devices.

Overcoming Challenges to a Safety-First Mindset

a. Complacency

- **Issue:** Experienced boaters may overlook safety precautions due to familiarity.
- **Solution:** Reinforce the importance of safety measures, regardless of experience level.

b. Resistance from Passengers

- **Issue:** Some passengers may view safety rules as unnecessary or inconvenient.
- **Solution:** Explain the rationale behind safety practices and involve passengers in drills.

c. Time Constraints

- **Issue:** Busy schedules may discourage thorough safety preparations.
- **Solution:** Integrate safety checks and briefings into the routine to make them efficient and non-negotiable.

Benefits of a Safety-First Mindset

Fewer Accidents:

- Prevents common emergencies caused by negligence or poor preparation.

Improved Confidence:

- Passengers and crew feel more secure knowing that safety is a priority.

Legal Compliance:

- Adherence to safety regulations reduces liability in case of an accident.

Enhanced Reputation:

- Boaters who prioritize safety earn the trust and respect of their peers and authorities.

Conclusion

- Encouraging a safety-first mindset is essential for preventing boating emergencies and ensuring the well-being of everyone onboard.
- By promoting education, preparation, and accountability, boaters can create a culture of safety that minimizes risks and enhances enjoyment.
- Safety is not just a responsibility but a shared value that protects lives and fosters trust among crew and passengers.

PART FOUR

MECHANICAL FAILURES

CHAPTER 16

ADDRESSING MECHANICAL FAILURES

Mechanical failures, particularly engine and steering issues, are among the most common boating emergencies. This checklist provides a structured step-by-step approach to diagnosing and resolving mechanical failures to ensure safety and restore functionality.

Initial Safety Measures

1. **Stop and Anchor**
   - Turn off the engine immediately to prevent further damage.
   - Drop anchor to secure the boat and maintain position.

2. **Ensure Passenger Safety**
   - Verify all passengers are safe and wearing life jackets, especially in rough conditions.

- Contact nearby vessels or the Coast Guard if assistance is required.

3. **Inspect the Surroundings**
   - Look for visible hazards such as debris, shallow water, or obstacles that may have caused the failure.

Checking the Propulsion System

A. Inspecting the Propeller

Procedure

1. Visually check for bent, chipped, or missing blades.
2. Rotate the propeller manually to check for smooth movement and obstructions.
   - Remove any fishing lines, seaweed, or debris wrapped around the shaft.

What to Look For

- Evenly shaped blades with no visible damage.
- Unrestricted, smooth rotation.

B. Examining the Propeller Shaft

Procedure

1. Inspect the shaft for signs of bending or wear.
2. Check the coupling at the engine to ensure it is secure.

What to Look For

- Straight, undamaged shaft.
- Secure and tight coupling.

Understanding the Steering System

Diagnosing Hydraulic Steering Failures

Check for Common Symptoms

- Difficulty turning the wheel or unresponsive steering.
- Fluid leaks or low hydraulic fluid levels.

Inspecting Hydraulic System Components

Helm Pump (Steering Wheel Assembly)

- Located behind the steering wheel on the console/dashboard.
- Ensure the pump is intact and turning the wheel generates pressure.
- Check for hydraulic fluid leaks around the pump and fittings.

Hydraulic Fluid Reservoir

- Typically integrated with the helm pump or mounted separately under the console.
- Check fluid levels and look for signs of contamination or leaks.

Hydraulic Hoses

- Running from the helm pump to the steering cylinder at the stern.
- Look for wear, cracks, or leaks along the lines.
- Ensure hoses are securely connected.

Steering Cylinder

- Mounted at the engine (outboard) or rudder (inboard).
- Check for leaks around seals and inspect piston movement.

Bleed Nipples

- Located on the steering cylinder.
- Use for bleeding air from the hydraulic system if steering feels spongy.

Addressing Hydraulic Fluid Loss & Steering Issues

Steps to Refill or Replace Hydraulic Fluid

1. Gather Necessary Tools and Materials

- Recommended hydraulic fluid (e.g., SeaStar or equivalent).
- Bleed kit (hoses and fittings).
- Wrenches, screwdrivers, clean rags, and a container for old fluid.

2. Prepare the System

- Secure the boat in a calm, stable area.
- Turn off the engine.
- Inspect for visible leaks before refilling.

3. Bleeding and Refilling Process

- Open bleed nipples on the steering cylinder.
- Slowly pour fluid into the helm pump reservoir while

turning the wheel fully left and right.

- Continue until air bubbles stop exiting the bleed hoses.
- Tighten bleed nipples and check fluid levels again.

4. Test the System

- Turn the wheel in both directions to ensure smooth operation.
- Inspect hoses, fittings, and components for leaks.
- Conduct a short test run to confirm proper steering function.

Preventing Hydraulic Fluid Loss

Routine Inspections

- Check hoses, seals, and fittings regularly for wear or damage.
- Monitor hydraulic fluid levels before every trip.

Scheduled Maintenance

- Replace old or damaged hoses and seals as needed.
- Flush and replace hydraulic fluid every 1–2 years.

Use Manufacturer-Recommended Fluids

- Avoid using improper hydraulic fluids that can damage seals and components.

Protect the System

- Avoid applying excessive force to the steering wheel.
- Ensure all hydraulic components are secured and undamaged.

Chapter 17

FUEL SYSTEMS

Checking Fuel Level

- Open the fuel tank cap and visually inspect the fuel level.
- For built-in tanks, check the dashboard fuel gauge.
- Use a dipstick or measuring tool for manual confirmation if the gauge is faulty.
- Ensure the fuel valve is open.
- Check for signs of water contamination in the fuel tank.

Inspecting Fuel Lines and Connections

- Look for cracks, bulges, or soft spots in fuel hoses from the tank to the engine.
- Check all hose connections for tightness and fuel leakage.
- Examine transparent fuel lines (if equipped) for air bubbles.

Chapter 18

FUEL FILTERS

Inspecting and Maintaining Fuel Filters

- Locate the primary Racor fuel filter (water separator).
- Locate the secondary fuel filter near the engine.
- Check the water separator bowl for accumulated water.
- Drain water and sediment from the bowl if necessary.
- Examine the filter element for dirt, clogging, or discoloration.
- Replace fuel filters as needed.

CHAPTER 19

FUEL CONTAMINATION

Common Signs of Engine Failure Due to Contaminated Marine Diesel Fuel

Engine Sputtering, Stalling, or Loss of Power
- Engine loses power under load, struggles to reach higher RPMs.
- Excessive Black or White Smoke from Exhaust
- Black Smoke: Poor combustion.
- White Smoke: Water or incomplete combustion.

Clogged Fuel Filters & Frequent Replacements
- Brown or black microbial slime clogs filters rapidly.

Difficulty Starting Engine or No Start
- Engine cranks but fails to fire or stalls immediately.

Unusual Engine Noise (Knocking or Rough Running)
- Excessive vibration or knocking sounds.

Water or Sludge in Fuel Samples

- Cloudy fuel, water droplets, dark sludge, sour smell.

Immediate Actions if Signs Occur

- Stop engine immediately to prevent further damage.
- Replace clogged fuel filters; inspect for contamination.
- Drain fuel-water separator; use biocide.
- Polish or drain severely contaminated fuel.
- Refuel from trusted source.

Preventing Future Contamination

- Use diesel biocide regularly.
- Drain fuel-water separator weekly.
- Keep tanks approximately 90% full.
- Use stabilizers for storage exceeding 6 months.
- Refuel from reputable marinas.

Marine Diesel Fuel Overview

Distillate Oils: Diesel (#2 Fuel Oil), Kerosene (#1), Heating Oils.

Types of Marine Diesel

- **Marine Gas Oil (MGO)**: Low viscosity, clean-burning.
- **Marine Diesel Oil (MDO)**: Medium viscosity, residual/distillate blend.
- **Intermediate Fuel Oil (IFO)**: Heavy/residual oil blend.
- **Heavy Fuel Oil (HFO)**: Very viscous, cheapest, high sulfur.

Environmental & IMO 2020 Regulations

- Global sulfur limit ≤0.5%; ECAs ≤0.1%.

Key Chemical Properties

- **Cetane Rating**: Higher = shorter ignition delay. Marine diesel CN ~40–50.
- **Viscosity & Density**: Marine diesel heavier, higher viscosity.
- **Sulfur Content & Regulations**: Marine diesel may have higher sulfur unless regulated.
- **Additives & Dye**: Marine diesel dyed red for tax purposes, fewer additives.

Differences: Marine vs. Regular Diesel

- **Regulatory & Sulfur Levels**: Marine diesel has higher sulfur outside regulated areas; automotive diesel strictly limited (15 ppm).
- **Formulation & Additives**: Marine diesel lacks detergents; automotive includes additives for performance.
- **Viscosity & Use Cases**: Marine heavier for slow-speed engines; automotive lighter for high-speed engines.
- **Legality & Compatibility**: Marine diesel (dyed) illegal for road use.

Diesel Fuel Breakdown Stages & Factors

- **0–6 Months (Fresh Fuel)**: Typically stable if properly stored.

- **6–12 Months (Beginning Breakdown)**: Mild oxidation, slight cetane drop.
- **12+ Months (Sludge Formation)**: Varnish, water accumulation, microbes.
- **2+ Years (Severe Degradation)**: Darkens, acidic, damaging.

Major Accelerating Factors

- Oxidation
- Water/Microbial Growth
- Sediment/Dirt/Rust

Fuel Maintenance & Lifespan Extension

Regular Treatment & Additives

- Biocide (every 3–6 months)
- Stabilizer (every 6–12 months)
- Cetane Booster (as needed)

Proper Storage

- Tanks ~90% full
- Sealed containers
- Rotate fuel every 6–12 months

Filtration & Water Removal

- Frequent filter changes
- Fuel polishing systems
- Clear bowl separators for visual inspection

Fuel Testing & Inspection

- Regular visual & microbial tests

Prevalence of Diesel Fuel Contamination (20–100 ft boats)

- **Contamination Statistics**: 50–70% of engine failures.
- **Why Common?**: Water intrusion, microbial growth, storage issues.
- **Consequences**: Filter clogs, injector damage, sudden engine shutdown.

Fuel Contamination Prevention Checklist

Fuel Selection & Bunkering

- Trusted marinas, high turnover.
- Small fuel sample testing.
- Portable filters during fueling.

Fuel Tank Maintenance

- Keep ≥90% full.
- Weekly water-separator draining.
- Regular biocide/stabilizer usage.

Filtration & Water Removal

- High-quality filters, regular replacements.
- Clear bowl separators.

Regular Fuel Testing

- Every 6 months: water, microbes, particulates.

Fuel Polishing Systems

- **When to Polish**: Fuel older than 6–12 months or visible contamination.
- **Types**: Onboard, portable, professional.
- **Steps**: Multi-stage filtration, biocide treatment, sludge disposal.

Diesel Fuel Biocides: What, Why, & How

Purpose of Biocides

- Kills/prevents microbial growth (bacteria, fungi, algae).
- Targets sludge that clogs filters, corrodes system components.

How Biocides Work

- Chemically destroy microbes in fuel + water layers.
- Break down sludge colonies for easier filtration.
- Protect against microbial-induced corrosion.

Popular Biocide Brands

- Biobor JF
- Power Service Bio Kleen
- Star Tron
- FPPF Killem
- Hammonds Biobor EB
- ValvTect Bioguard.

Biocide Usage

Preventative (every 3–6 months):

- Add recommended dose to fresh fuel before long storage.

Treatment (for active contamination):

- Double-dose per instructions; let it sit 12–48 hours.
- Expect frequent filter changes as dead microbes slough off.

Best Practices

- Follow exact dosing guidelines.
- Keep extra filters on board during treatments.

Key Takeaways

Multiple Contamination Points:

- Production, distribution, storage, transfer, and onboard handling all pose risk.

Marina Fuel Risks:

- Likelihood varies (5–50%+), influenced by tank upkeep, turnover rate, environmental factors, and fueling practices.

Prevention/Minimization:

- **Good fueling habits** (sample tests, reputable marinas).
- **Maintenance** (weekly water separator draining, filter changes).

- **Additives** (biocides, stabilizers) to combat microbes/oxidation.
- **Fuel polishing** if storing >6–12 months or detecting significant contamination.

Biocide & Polishing:

- **Biocides** kill microbes, essential for sludge-laden or water-contaminated fuel.
- **Polishing** reconditions older or contaminated diesel, removing water and sediment.

CHAPTER 20

ELECTRICAL SYSTEMS

Preventing Electrical & Ignition System Failures

Battery System Maintenance

Verify battery voltage with a multimeter:

- **12.6V+** (fully charged, engine off)
- **13.8V–14.4V** (charging, engine running)
    - Check battery terminals for corrosion and secure connections.
    - Ensure battery cables are properly insulated and not damaged.

Starter Solenoid Troubleshooting

- Listen for clicking sounds when turning the key (indicates solenoid issues).
- Check solenoid wiring for corrosion and loose connections.
- Test starter motor if the solenoid clicks but doesn't engage the engine.

Preventive Maintenance

- Regularly inspect the solenoid terminals for corrosion and clean if necessary.
- Check wiring connections to ensure a secure and clean electrical path.
- Test the battery and charging system periodically to prevent weak starts.
- Listen for early signs of failure, such as slow cranking or clicking sounds when starting the engine

Conclusion

Understanding how to diagnose and troubleshoot propulsion, steering, fuel, and ignition failures is crucial for safe boating. Regular maintenance and inspections will help prevent emergencies, ensuring a smooth and controlled boating experience. Always refer to the manufacturer's manual for specific guidance on your boat's systems.

For additional AI-powered troubleshooting and expert guidance, check out Hix AI Chat – the best ChatGPT alternative for all your boating needs!

CHAPTER 21

DC BATTERY SYSTEMS, POWER DISTRIBUTION AND CHARGING SYSTEMS

Power Distribution: Breaker Panels and Fuse Boxes

- The **main breaker panel** distributes power and includes labeled switches and breakers for various systems.
- **Fuse boxes** protect circuits by breaking the connection if current exceeds safe limits.
- Fuses are located near critical systems and come in types like blade and ANL/T-class.
- **Wiring** must be color-coded, marine-grade, corrosion-resistant, and well-insulated.

Charging the Battery System

- The **alternator** charges batteries using engine power (typically 12.2–12.14V DC).
- **Shore power** charges batteries through a charger/converter when docked.

- **Solar panels and wind generators** provide supplementary DC charging using renewable energy.

Inverters: Converting DC to AC Power

- An **inverter** converts 12V/24V DC to 120V/240V AC for appliances.
- **Pure sine wave inverters** are ideal for sensitive electronics.
- **Modified sine wave inverters** are more affordable but may cause issues with sensitive devices.
- **Inverters** allow use of AC appliances without shore power or a generator.
- **Inverter/charger combos** switch automatically between shore and battery power and charge batteries.

AC Power System (If Equipped)

- **Shore power connections** power systems or charge batteries and include safety features:
  - Reverse polarity indicators
  - Circuit breakers
- **Generators** on larger yachts produce AC power for heavy or extended loads.

Protective Components: Fuses and Circuit Breakers

- **Fuses** protect circuits and must be regularly inspected and replaced with correct ratings.
- **Circuit breakers** auto-disconnect during overloads and are found in panels and near key devices.

Power Consumers (Loads)

- **Essential systems** (DC-powered):
  - ○ Navigation lights
  - ○ Bilge pumps
  - ○ Communication systems (VHF, GPS)
- **Non-essential systems** (AC-powered):
  - ○ Appliances (TVs, A/C)
  - ○ Lighting (preferably energy-efficient LEDs)

Monitoring and Safety

- **Battery monitoring systems** track voltage, current, and charge levels to avoid over-discharge.
- **Grounding and bonding** prevent electrical faults and corrosion.
- Regular **maintenance** includes inspecting wiring, cleaning terminals, and testing components.

Chain of Events Summary

- Batteries store DC power.
- Distribution through breakers and fuses protects and allocates power.
- Charging occurs via alternators, shore power, or renewables.
- Inverters convert DC to AC for appliances.
- Loads include essential (DC) and non-essential (AC) systems.
- Monitoring and safety ensure system reliability and longevity.

Conclusion

A boat's electrical system integrates DC and AC components to power systems safely and efficiently, requiring regular monitoring and maintenance for optimal performance.

CHAPTER 22

WHEN AN ENGINE WON'T START

Check the Electrical System

Use a **multimeter** to test battery voltage.
- Fully charged: ~12.14V (engine off)
- Charging: ~13.8–14.4V (engine running)

Determine the Voltage and Current Rating of a Multimeter

- Understand ratings to avoid damage or hazards during use.

Look for Information on the Multimeter

- **Label on the device**: Check near ports or on the back for:
  - Max voltage rating (e.g., 1400V)
  - Max current rating (e.g., 10A or 20A)

- **Symbols and units**:
  - ◦ AC Voltage: V~ (wavy line)
  - ◦ DC Voltage: V– (straight line with dots)
  - ◦ AC Current: A~
  - ◦ DC Current: A–

- **Port labels**:
  - ◦ COM = common (black probe)
  - ◦ V/Ω/mA = voltage/resistance/small current
  - ◦ 10A = high-current measurements

- **Check the multimeter's manual** for:
  - ◦ Max voltage and current
  - ◦ Input impedance
  - ◦ Safety category (CAT I–IV)

Inspect Fuse Ratings

- Internal fuses protect current measurement circuits.
- Check and match **voltage and current** ratings before replacement.

Test the Multimeter with Known Values

- Begin with low-energy circuits before attempting higher voltage/current.

Safety Tips for Operation

- Never exceed the voltage/current ratings.
- Use the correct port and range setting.
- Use a CAT-rated multimeter appropriate for your environment.

CHAPTER 23

IGNITION SYSTEMS

Testing the Ignition System

- Remove and inspect spark plugs (look for fouling, wear, oil).
- Ground the plug, crank the engine, and check for a **blue spark**.

Fuses, Wiring, Solenoid, and Starter

- Inspect and replace blown fuses (match rating).
- Check for loose, corroded, or frayed wires.
- Verify spark plug wire connections.

Solenoid Role and Replacement

- Solenoid engages the starter and acts as a high-current relay.
- Can be **separate** or **integrated** in the starter motor.
- Replacement considerations:
  - Part availability

- ° Cost-effectiveness
- ° Starter motor condition

Steps to Replace a Solenoid

- Disconnect the battery.
- Access and remove the solenoid.
- Install the new solenoid and reconnect wiring.
- Test the starter system.

Signs the Solenoid Needs Replacement

- Clicking sound, no crank.
- No sound when starting.
- Intermittent starts or corroded terminals.

Starter System Troubleshooting

- Battery test: ≥12.14V.
- Inspect connections.
- Listen for clicking (test solenoid).
- Bypass solenoid with jumper cable.
- Bench test starter if needed.

Coil System in Diesel Engines

- Check glow plugs, relays, sensors, and ECU.
- Use multimeter for resistance tests.
- Scan ECU for error codes.

General Ignition Diagnosis

- Listen for clicks, check dash lights.
- Load test the battery.
- Test fuel delivery system if ignition is functional but engine won't start.

Chapter 24

COOLING SYSTEMS

Marine engines rely on cooling systems to prevent overheating and ensure optimal performance. These systems use either raw water directly or a closed-loop coolant system with a heat exchanger. Below is a comprehensive guide to components, troubleshooting, and maintenance.

Cooling System Components

Water Intake

- Draw raw water from sea/lake/river.
- Use **strainer** to filter out debris like seaweed, sand, or trash.
- Inspect intake port regularly for obstruction.

Water Pump and Impeller

- Impeller-driven pump circulates water through the system.

- Impeller must be flexible and intact for efficient flow.
- Inspect pump for leaks, cracks, or corrosion.
- Replace impeller every 1–2 years or if damaged.
- Test for strong, steady water flow.

Heat Exchanger (Closed-Loop Systems Only)

- Transfers heat from engine coolant to raw water without mixing.
- Provides better corrosion protection than raw water systems.
- Inspect for leaks (look for coolant mixing with raw water).
- Flush regularly to prevent scale buildup.
- Maintain proper coolant levels.

Engine Cooling Passages

- **Raw Water Cooling**: Water flows directly through engine passages.
- **Closed-Loop**: Coolant circulates internally and is cooled via heat exchanger.
- Monitor temperature gauge for proper flow.
- Flush with fresh water after saltwater use.
- Check for corrosion or clogs, especially in saltwater environments.

Thermostat Regulation

- Opens only when engine reaches operating temperature.
- Regulates water flow to maintain optimal engine temp.

- Replace every 2–3 years or if malfunctioning.
- Monitor engine temperature to prevent overheating or cold running.

Exhaust Manifold Cooling

- Cooled water flows into the exhaust manifold.
- Mixes with exhaust gases to reduce temperature before discharge.
- Inspect for blockages (soot, salt deposits).
- Watch for steam or unusual smoke—may indicate cooling failure.

Outflow & Discharge

- Expels cooled water and exhaust overboard.
- Look for a visible, steady stream ("tell-tale").
- Monitor for weak/no flow or unusual sounds (gurgling, excessive steam).

Flow Summary

1. Water Intake
2. Pump/Impeller
3. Heat Exchanger (if applicable)
4. Engine Cooling Passages
5. Thermostat
6. Exhaust Manifold
7. Overboard Discharge

Types of Marine Cooling Systems

- **Raw Water Cooling**: Simpler, direct water flow; less corrosion protection.
- **Closed-Loop Cooling**: Uses coolant and heat exchanger; more complex but better protection

Signs of Cooling Problems

- Engine overheating
- Weak or no water flow
- Clogged strainer or intake
- Damaged impeller (cracks, missing blades)
- Leaking heat exchanger (coolant mixing with raw water)

Routine Maintenance Tips

- Clean strainer regularly
- Replace impeller every 1–2 years
- Replace thermostat every 2–3 years
- Flush system with fresh water after saltwater use
- Check coolant levels (closed-loop systems)
- Inspect outflow for steady discharge

Conclusion

The marine engine cooling system follows a precise sequence—from water intake to heat absorption and discharge. Each component, from the impeller to the thermostat, plays a vital role in regulating temperature. Regular inspection and preventive maintenance are key to long-term engine efficiency and reliability.

CHAPTER 25

ENGINE OVERHEATING

Marine Engine Overheating & Thermostat Testing Checklist

This checklist provides a structured approach to diagnosing and resolving marine engine overheating issues, with a focus on thermostat testing and cooling system maintenance.

Coolant Level Inspection

- Ensure the Coolant Reservoir is Full (Check fluid level against tank markings).
- Look for Leaks (Inspect hoses, radiator cap, and connections).
- Procedure:
    1. Open the coolant reservoir cap (only when the engine is cool).
    2. Check fluid levels and top up if needed.
    3. Inspect for leaks in hoses or around the reservoir.

- ° **What to Look For:** Adequate coolant level and no visible leaks.

Tools & Materials Needed for Thermostat Testing

- Wrenches or screwdrivers (to remove thermostat housing).
- Thermometer (reads up to 200°F/100°C).
- Container or saucepan (for hot water testing).
- Heat source (stove or hot plate).
- Clean water.
- Rags or towels (to clean up spills).
- New gasket or O-ring (if needed for reassembly).

Removing & Inspecting the Thermostat

- Turn Off the Engine (Ensure it's completely cool).
- Locate the Thermostat (Refer to engine manual for exact location).
- Drain the Cooling System (Open the coolant drain plug or remove a nearby hose).
- Remove the Thermostat Housing (Use wrench or screwdriver to loosen bolts).
- Inspect the Thermostat (Check for corrosion, damage, or debris).
- Replace if Necessary (If the thermostat appears damaged, replace it instead of testing).

Testing the Thermostat in Hot Water

- **Prepare the Water:**
    - ° Fill a container or saucepan with water.
    - ° Heat the water slowly and monitor

temperature with a thermometer.

- **Submerge the Thermostat in the Water** (Avoid contact with container bottom).
- **Observe the Thermostat's Operation**
  - ○ **Opening Temperature:** The thermostat should begin to open at its rated temperature (e.g., 120°F/49°C or 140°F/60°C).
  - ○ **Fully Open Temperature:** Continue heating and ensure the thermostat fully opens as the temperature rises.
- **Cooling Test:**
  - ○ Remove container from heat and allow water to cool gradually.
  - ○ The thermostat should **close fully** as the temperature drops below its rated opening temperature.
- **Compare to Specifications** (Check engine manual for correct opening/closing temperatures).
- **Replace if Necessary** (If the thermostat fails to open/close properly or operates outside specifications.)

Reinstalling the Thermostat

- Clean the Thermostat Housing (Remove old gasket material or debris).
- Insert the Thermostat (Ensure correct orientation—spring side facing the engine).
- Install a New Gasket or O-Ring (To ensure a proper seal).
- Reattach the Housing (Tighten bolts evenly to prevent leaks).
- Refill the Cooling System (Top up with fresh coolant or raw water and bleed air from the system).

Testing the System After Reassembly

- Start the Engine (Let it warm up while monitoring temperature gauge).
- Check for Proper Operation:
    - Engine should reach and maintain normal operating temperature.
    - Water should flow properly through the cooling system.
- Inspect for Leaks (Check thermostat housing and coolant hoses).

Symptoms of a Faulty Thermostat

- **Stuck Open:**
    - Engine runs too cool, reducing efficiency.
    - Carbon buildup due to inefficient combustion.
    - Delayed or weak cabin heating (for boats with heating systems).
- **Stuck Closed:**
    - Rapid engine overheating, risking severe damage.
    - Little or no water flow from cooling system outflow.

Thermostat Maintenance Tips

- Test the Thermostat Annually (Part of regular engine maintenance).
- Replace Every 2–3 Years (Or as specified in the engine's maintenance schedule).
- Use Manufacturer-Recommended Thermostats (Ensure proper fit and function).

Conclusion

A faulty thermostat can lead to inefficient engine performance or severe overheating issues. Regular inspections, proper testing, and timely replacements will help maintain optimal cooling system function.

Chapter 26

UNDERSTANDING THE IMPELLER IN MARINE COOLING SYSTEMS

Marine Cooling System Impeller Inspection & Maintenance Checklist

The impeller is a critical component of a boat's cooling system, ensuring proper water circulation to prevent engine overheating. This checklist provides a structured approach to inspecting, maintaining, and replacing the impeller.

Role of the Impeller in the Cooling System

- **Pumps Raw Water into the System (Draws water from the lake, river, or ocean).**
- **Maintains Engine Temperature (Ensures continuous cooling).**
- **Supplies Water to Exhaust Cooling (Prevents overheating of exhaust components).**

How the Impeller Works

- Rotates Inside the Pump **(Mounted on a shaft and spins with engine operation).**
- Creates a Vacuum **(Flexible blades collapse and expand to draw in water).**
- Pushes Water Through the System **(Ensures steady water flow to the engine).**

Signs of a Faulty Impeller

- Reduced or No Water Flow **(Check "tell-tale" stream exiting the boat).**
- Engine Overheating **(Temperature warning alarms).**
- Unusual Noises **(Grinding or whining from the water pump area).**
- Visible Blade Damage **(Cracks, tears, or missing impeller fins).**

Maintenance & Replacement Schedule

- Inspect Annually **(Look for signs of wear and damage).**
- Replace Every 2–3 Years **(Even if it appears in good condition).**
- Flush the Cooling System **(After every use, especially in saltwater).**

Steps to Inspect & Replace the Impeller

Gather Necessary Tools

- Screwdrivers or socket wrench.

- Needle-nose pliers.
- Replacement gasket or O-ring.
- Marine grease.
- Work gloves.
- Engine manual (for specific instructions).

Locating the Impeller

- Refer to the Engine Manual (**Find the impeller's location**).
- Identify the Water Pump Housing (**Usually near the lower unit of an outboard or front of an inboard engine**).

Access the Impeller

- Turn Off the Engine (**Ensure it's cool and disconnected from power**).
- Drain the Water (**If necessary, remove the cooling water drain plug**).
- Remove the Housing Cover (**Loosen bolts securing the water pump**).
- Extract the Impeller (**Gently pull it out using needle-nose pliers**).

Inspect the Impeller

- Check for Cracks, Tears, or Missing Blades (**Damaged impellers must be replaced**).
- Test Blade Flexibility (**Brittle or stiff blades indicate aging**).
- Inspect the Housing for Wear (**Look for corrosion or scoring inside the pump**).

- Examine the Keyway and Shaft **(Ensure they are intact and properly seated).**

Repair or Replace the Impeller

When to Replace

- If blades are worn, cracked, or broken.
- If the impeller is stiff or brittle.
- If engine overheating or reduced water flow is observed.

Installing a New Impeller

- Apply Marine Grease **(Coat impeller blades and housing lightly).**
- Align the Keyway **(Ensure proper fit on the shaft).**
- Compress the Blades **(Rotate and insert into housing, bending blades in the correct direction).**
- Secure the Housing Cover (Use a new gasket or O-ring for sealing).

Testing the New Impeller

- Reassemble the System **(Ensure all bolts and hoses are securely attached).**
- Start the Engine **(Run at idle in water or use a flushing attachment).**
- Check for Proper Water Flow **(Observe "tell-tale" stream or exhaust outlet).**
- Monitor for Leaks **(Inspect housing and connections).**

Maintenance Tips for Longevity

- Inspect Annually **(Especially in sandy or muddy environments).**
- Flush with Fresh Water **(After each use to remove debris and salt).**
- Replace Every 2–3 Years **(Even if no visible damage is present).**

PART FIVE

WEATHER-RELATED BOATING EMERGENCIES

Chapter 27

CAUGHT IN A STORM

This checklist provides essential steps for identifying, preventing, and responding to common weather-related boating emergencies.

Common Weather-Related Emergencies & Responses

Sudden Storms

- **Indicators:** Darkening skies, sudden temperature drops, shifting wind direction.
- **Risks:** Loss of visibility, capsizing, increased collision risk.
- **Response:**
  - Reduce speed and head into waves at a **45-degree angle**.
  - Secure all loose items and ensure passengers are safe.

○   Turn on navigation lights for visibility.

High Winds & Rough Seas

- **Indicators:** Sudden gusts, whitecaps forming on waves, strong opposing currents.
- **Risks:** Capsizing, loss of control, difficulty navigating.
- **Response:**
    - ○   Adjust throttle to match conditions.
    - ○   Shift weight to maintain stability.
    - ○   Avoid perpendicular waves; approach them at an angle.

Fog

- **Indicators:** Sudden visibility drop, thick mist appearing.
- **Risks:** Collisions with other boats, land, or obstacles.
- **Response:**
    - ○   Reduce speed and proceed cautiously.
    - ○   Use radar, GPS, and foghorns to signal presence.
    - ○   Anchor if necessary, until visibility improves.

Lightning Storms

- **Indicators:** Increasing thunder, flashes of lightning, electric charge in the air.
- **Risks:** Electrical system damage, personal injury from strikes.
- **Response:**
    - ○   Head to shore if possible.
    - ○   Disconnect all electronics and avoid metal surfaces.

　　　° Stay low in the boat to minimize exposure.

Tornadoes or Waterspouts

- **Indicators:** Funnel-shaped cloud extending from sky to water.
- **Risks:** Vessel damage, capsizing, extreme winds.
- **Response:**
  - ° Steer clear of the tornado's path.
  - ° Head for shore or deeper water, depending on conditions.
  - ° Secure all passengers and prepare for rough waves.

Cold Weather & Hypothermia Risks

- **Indicators:** Extremely low air temperatures, icy water, strong wind chills.
- **Risks:** Rapid heat loss, life-threatening hypothermia.
- **Response:**
  - ° Wear insulated, waterproof gear.
  - ° Avoid prolonged water exposure.
  - ° Keep dry and warm in emergency situations.

Preventing Weather-Related Emergencies

1. Pre-Trip Weather Checks

- Monitor marine weather forecasts before departure.
- Look for small craft advisories, wind warnings, or storms.
- Avoid boating in unstable weather conditions.

2. Use of Navigation Tools

- Equip the boat with radar, GPS, and marine weather radio.
- Learn how to interpret tide charts and weather reports.

3. Plan Alternative Routes

- Identify safe harbors and anchorages along your planned route.
- Have backup routes in case of emergency.

4. Carry Essential Equipment:

- Life jackets for all passengers.
- Flares, whistles, and signaling devices.
- Weatherproof VHF radio for emergency communication.

Responding to Weather-Related Emergencies

1. Stay Calm

- Panic leads to poor decision-making. Focus on stabilizing the boat.

2. Reduce Speed

- Slower speeds help maintain control and minimize wave impact.

3. Secure the Boat & Passengers

- Close hatches and secure loose items.
- Ensure all passengers are seated and wearing life jackets.

4. Communicate with Authorities

- Use a VHF radio to notify nearby vessels and the Coast Guard.

- Provide location and nature of the emergency.

5. Navigate Safely

- Steer into waves at an angle to prevent capsizing.
- Follow marked channels to avoid shallow areas or obstacles.

Emergency Communication

VHF Radio Protocol:

- Use **Channel 16** for distress calls.
- Clearly state your boat's name, location, and nature of distress.

Distress Signals:

- Use flares, smoke signals, or flashing lights in low visibility conditions.

Emergency Beacon (EPIRB):

- Activate the Emergency Position-Indicating Radio Beacon if in serious danger.

Survival Tips for Severe Weather

If Capsizing Occurs

- Stay with the boat—it's easier to spot than an individual in the water.
- Climb onto the overturned hull if possible to prevent hypothermia.

Dealing with Prolonged Storms

- Conserve energy and rations.
- Maintain radio contact with rescuers or nearby boats.

Sheltering in Place

- Drop anchor in a safe area if navigation is impossible.

Conclusion

Weather-related boating emergencies require preparation, vigilance, and quick decision-making. By staying informed, equipping your vessel properly, and remaining calm in critical situations,

Chapter 28

RESPONDING TO WEATHER EMERGENCIES

High Winds and Rough Seas

Angle the Bow (Approx. 30°–45° to Waves)
- Avoid heading into waves directly or letting the boat drift broadside.
- Maintain enough engine power to control movement.

Slow Down
- Reduce speed to prevent slamming into waves and maintain better maneuverability.

Trim the Boat
- Keep the bow slightly up (use trim tabs/hydrofoil if available) to minimize water washing over the deck.

Manage Water Ingress
- Continuously run bilge pumps.

- Seal hatches/doors to prevent further flooding.

Steer Clear of Hazardous Areas

- Avoid shallow waters, reef zones, or rocky coastlines where wave breaks intensify.

Key Point: Safe navigation in high winds involves controlled speed, correct bow angle to waves, and vigilant trimming to maintain stability.

Navigating in Fog
(Referencing COLREGS / Rules for Restricted Visibility)

Sound Signals (Rule 35)

- **Powerboats Making Way**: 1 prolonged blast every 2 mins.
- **Powerboats Stopped**: 2 prolonged blasts every 2 mins.
- **Sailing Vessels**: 1 prolonged + 2 short blasts every 2 mins.
- **Vessel at Anchor**: Rapid bell ringing for ~5 seconds every minute; if >100m, also ring a gong.

Use Navigation Lights (Rule 20)

- All vessels must have functioning nav lights in fog for visibility.

Proper Lookout (Rule 5)

- Assign a dedicated lookout using sight, hearing, radar for hazards.
- Slow down and be ready to change course or stop if needed.

Radar Usage

- If equipped, use radar to detect vessels/buoys/landmasses hidden by fog.

Best Practices

- **Reduce Speed** and be ready to maneuver/stop.
- **Use Horn/Bell** for appropriate signals.
- **Continuously Monitor** environment (sound, radar, radio traffic).
- **Adhere to Rule 19**: Vessels in restricted visibility must proceed with extreme caution.

Lightning Safety

What to Do During Lightning

1. Wear Life Jackets

- Ensure everyone has a PFD on in case of sudden impact or if thrown overboard.

2. Move to Safe Area

- If cabin available, stay inside, away from metal/electronics.
- In open boats, stay low in the center, minimize contact with metal.

3. Install Lightning Protection

- Grounding system or lightning rod directs strikes safely overboard.

4. Turn Off/Unplug Electronics

- Prevent surge damage; keep essential comms (VHF, EPIRB) available but limit usage.

5. Seek Shelter or Anchor

- If possible, find a safe harbor.
- If not, anchor in a safe spot away from tall objects.

What NOT to Do During Lightning

1. **Don't stay on elevated surfaces** or hold metal rods.
2. **Don't touch metal** (railings, steering wheel) during strikes.
3. **Don't use electronics** unless necessary for emergency comms.
4. **Don't remain in open water** as the tallest object.

If Lightning Strikes Your Boat

- Check for injuries, call for assistance.
- Inspect boat for damage/leaks; keep bilge pumps running if needed.

Key Takeaways for Lightning Safety

High Winds & Rough Seas

- Keep the bow angled to waves (~30°–45°), reduce speed, trim for stability, and continuously pump out water.

Fog Navigation

- Use correct **sound signals** per COLREGS, maintain **navigation lights**, reduce speed, use **radar** if available, and keep a **sharp lookout**.

Lightning Safety

- Wear PFDs, stay **low and away** from metal, **ground** the boat if possible, unplug non-essential electronics, and seek **safe harbor** or anchor if you can't outrun the storm.

PART SIX

OTHER EMERGENCIES

Chapter 29

CAPSIZING AND GROUNDING

How to Handle a Capsized Boat

General Principles for All Boats
That Have Capsized

1. Stay Calm and Assess the Situation: Take a moment to assess everyone's safety and the condition of the boat.

- Perform a headcount to ensure no one is missing.

2. Stay With the Boat: Unless it is drifting toward a dangerous area, stay close to the capsized vessel. It provides buoyancy, is easier to spot by rescuers, and can often be righted.

3. Signal for Help: Use available signaling devices such as flares, whistles, or an EPIRB (Emergency Position Indicating Radio Beacon).

- Wave arms, life jackets, or bright objects to attract attention.

4. Minimize Energy Use: Conserve energy and body heat, especially in cold water, to avoid hypothermia.

Small Boats (Kayaks, Canoes, Dinghies, etc.)

1. **Right the Boat:** Small boats are often easier to flip back upright. Swim to the boat's side, grab the gunwale (edge), and pull it toward you while kicking your legs.

2. **Re-Enter the Boat:** Once the boat is upright, climb in carefully to avoid tipping it over again.

3. **Bail Out Water:** Use a manual bilge pump, bucket, or even hands to remove water.

Precautions:
- Always wear a personal flotation device (PFD).
- Avoid overloading the boat, which can make it more prone to capsizing.

Large Boats (Sailboats, Motorboats, Yachts)
1. **Stay With the Boat:** Large boats may not sink completely, as many are designed with built-in flotation. Climb onto the hull or any part of the boat that remains above water.
2. **Signal for Help:** Activate an EPIRB, use flares, or call for help on a VHF radio.
3. **Do Not Attempt to Right Large Boats:** Righting a large, capsized boat without proper equipment is almost impossible. Focus on staying safe and awaiting rescue.

4. **Deploy Life raft or Flotation Devices:** If available, deploy a life raft or throw life rings to passengers.

Specific Situations:

- **Sailboats:** Use the mast leverage technique for smaller boats; for larger ones, stay on the overturned hull and await rescue.
- **Motorboats:** Stay on the capsized hull; these boats are not easily righted without professional assistance.

Cold Water Survival

The Huddle Position (If with Others)

1. **Form a Tight Group:** Keep bodies close together to minimize heat loss
2. **Wrap Arms Around Each Other:** Securely connect by placing arms over shoulders or under arms.
3. **Tuck Your Legs:** Pull knees to your chest to protect vital organs.
4. **Keep Heads Together:** Minimize exposed surface area to cold air and water.

The HELP Position (If Alone)

1. **Keep Your Body Tight:** Draw knees to chest, cross arms against chest to protect vital organs.
2. **Stay Still:** Avoid unnecessary movement to conserve energy.
3. **Keep Your Face Above Water:** Tilt head back slightly to keep mouth and nose above water.
4. **Float in a Compact Shape:** Reduce surface area exposure to cold water.

Key Considerations:

- Ensure everyone wears life jackets for buoyancy.
- Stay calm and avoid unnecessary movement to reduce heat loss.
- Do not break the huddle until rescue arrives.

Grounding

Preventing Grounding:

- When in unfamiliar waters, call the nearest **Boat US** or **Sea Tow** for navigation guidance.
- Use navigation charts and GPS to monitor depth.
- Slow down in shallow waters to minimize damage if grounding occurs.

Steps to Take When Grounding Occurs

1. **Stay Calm and Assess the Situation:** Check for injuries among passengers.
2. **Stop the Engines:** Shut off immediately to prevent further damage.
3. **Inspect for Damage:** Look for leaks, cracks, or visible damage.
4. **Secure the Boat:** Drop an anchor to prevent drifting into more hazardous areas.

Handling a Small Boat Grounding

1. **Shift Weight:** Move passengers and gear to the side furthest from the grounding point.
2. **Push Off:** Use a pole or paddle to push the boat free.
3. **Reverse Slowly:** Use the engine in reverse at low throttle if safe to do so.
4. **Check the Hull:** Once free, inspect for cracks or breaches.

Handling a Large Boat Grounding

1. **Shift Ballast and Weight:** Redistribute weight to reduce draft.
2. **Use the Engine Cautiously:** Attempt to reverse at low power.
3. **Deploy a Kedge Anchor:** Use an anchor in deeper water to help pull the boat free.
4. **Call for Tow Assistance:** If unable to free the boat, contact professional towing services.

If the Boat Is Stuck or Damaged:

1. Inspect for leaks or flooding and activate bilge pumps.
2. Avoid further damage by securing the boat.
3. Notify authorities using a **VHF radio** or **emergency beacon**.
4. Evacuate if sinking or capsizing is imminent.

Communicating with Rescue Services

1. Contact the Coast Guard: Use **VHF Marine Radio Channel 16** or **Channel 114 (International).**

   a. **Provide a Clear Distress Call.** Include:

      i. Nature of the emergency (capsizing, grounding, injury, etc.).

      ii. Location (latitude, longitude, or description).

      iii. Number of people on board.

      iv. Any immediate dangers (injuries, flooding, risk of sinking).

2. Contact Local Marine Authorities

3. Use Emergency Beacons: Activate **EPIRB** or **PLB** if VHF is unavailable.

4. Signal Nearby Vessels: Use flares, flags, or sound signals to attract attention.

5. Notify Emergency Services: If within phone range, dial **911** or **1-800-DAD-SAFE** for Coast Guard assistance in the U.S.

6. Use Marine Rescue Apps: SafeTrx, USCG Boating Safety App, or local **Boat US/Sea Tow** apps can send automated distress calls.

7. Inform Your Float Plan Contact: Ensure someone onshore is aware of your route and estimated arrival times.

By following this structured checklist, you can improve response and survival chances during a boating emergency. Always prioritize safety and be prepared for unexpected situations.

Chapter 30

DEMASTING

Definition and Frequency

Demasting

- Catastrophic failure or loss of a boat's mast
- Leaves sailboat without primary propulsion
- Serious maritime emergency, infrequent for well-maintained vessels

Statistical Frequency

- Exact global stats unavailable
- More common in competitive/offshore racing
- Less frequent for recreational sailors; linked to poor maintenance/weather misjudgment

Most Common Causes of Demasting

Rigging Failure (Most Common Cause)

- Standing Rigging (shrouds, stays, chainplates):

Metal fatigue, corrosion, improper tension, broken turnbuckles
- Running Rigging (halyards, sheets): Wear, UV damage, inspection neglect
- Neglect: Poor maintenance

Extreme Weather Conditions

- High winds, sudden squalls, rough seas
- Failing to reef or reduce sail

Human Error

- Overloading sails
- Improper handling (tacking/jibing, reefing)
- Mishandling running backstays

Structural Weakness in Mast/Components

- Internal cracks, corrosion, prior impacts
- Poor design or under spec'd masts

Collision or Impact

- Overhead obstructions (bridge/tree limb)
- Collision with other vessels/docks/submerged objects
- Grounding stress on rigging

Age of the Boat

- Older vessels more prone to rigging fatigue
- Neglected upgrades amplify risk

Competitive Sailing Stresses

- Racing maneuvers in extreme conditions

Improper Mast Step or Base
- Mast not seated/aligned properly
- Failing mast collars or base hardware

Manufacturing Defects (Rare)
- Material/design flaws

Immediate Dangers of Demasting

Loss of Propulsion
- Reliance on auxiliary engine or drift

Crew Safety Risks
- Falling mast parts, tangled rigging, sharp debris

Capsizing Hazard
- Dragging mast destabilizes boat

Hull Damage
- Broken mast/rigging can puncture hull or deck

Entanglement
- Rigging catching underwater obstacles

Prevention of Demasting

Rigging Maintenance & Inspection
- Regular corrosion/wear checks
- Replace standing rigging every 7–10 years

- Maintain running rigging

Weather Preparedness

- Reduce sail area early
- Monitor forecasts; avoid extremes

Proper Handling

- Correct sailing maneuvers training

Upgrades & Repairs

- Use high-quality rigging/mast materials
- Professional repairs

Routine Surveys

- Professional inspections regularly

Emergency Response to Demasting

Ensure Crew Safety

- Move crew from debris
- Provide first aid

Stabilize the Vessel

- Cut away/secure mast and rigging
- Balance boat

Assess Damage

- Inspect hull/deck integrity

Establish Propulsion

- Auxiliary engine
- Jury rig if necessary

Notify Authorities

- VHF radio Channel 16
- Provide location, damage, crew condition

Navigate Safely

- Head to safe harbor or repair point

Jury Rigging After Demasting

Temporary Rig Setup

- Boom/spinnaker pole as mast
- Spare lines/halyards to secure smaller sail
- Lash to stable points

Stabilize & Balance

- Brace tension lines properly
- Test steering/sail balance

Alternative Propulsion

- Motor or arrange a tow

Rigging Maintenance Checklist

Visual Inspection (Monthly/Pre-Sail)

- Standing rigging for corrosion/cracks

- Running rigging wear/frays
- Mast/boom integrity

Cleaning (Quarterly/Post-Harsh Conditions)

- Rinse with fresh water
- Lubricate blocks/sheaves/turnbuckles

Standing Rigging Maintenance (Annually)

- Inspect chainplates, tension rigging
- Lubricate/align spreaders

Running Rigging Maintenance (Annually)

- Replace halyards/sheets if worn
- Wash ropes, replace hardware

Mast & Spar Maintenance (Annually)

- Thorough inspection, repaint corrosion
- Lubricate sheaves

Fittings & Hardware (Annually)

- Inspect cleats, winches, organizers
- Replace cracked fittings, tighten screws

Specialized Rigging Checks (2–3 Years)

- Professional inspections
- Replace standing rigging every 7–10 years

Safety Checks (Pre-Sail)

- Verify pins, rings, rigging order
- Test raising/reefing/lowering sails

Tools & Supplies

- Lubricants, cotter pins, rigging tape
- Wire cutters, spare hardware

Documentation

- Maintenance log of inspections/repairs

Rigging Maintenance Summary

Documentation

- Maintenance log for inspections/repairs
- Record rigging settings

Halyards vs. Sheets

- **Halyard:** Hoists/lowers sails vertically
- **Sheet:** Controls horizontal sail angle

Jury Rigging & Emergency Repair Kit

Preparing a Jury Rig

- Secure vessel from further damage
- Boom/pole as mast, smaller sail
- Lash securely to deck points
- Create temporary shrouds/stays
- Adjust sail trim minimally for control

Preparing an Emergency Repair Kit

- Essential tools (multi-tool, wire cutters)
- Spare rigging materials (rope, shackles)
- Fasteners (epoxy, zip ties, clamps)

- Safety gear (gloves, first aid kit)
- Documentation/reference diagrams

Tips for Successful Jury Rigging

- Practice beforehand
- Prioritize crew safety
- Aim for functionality, not perfection

Key Takeaways

Definition & Causes

- Demasting from rigging failure, weather, human error
- Proper maintenance significantly reduces risk

Immediate Dangers

- Loss of propulsion, crew injury, capsizing, hull damage

Emergency Response

- Stabilize crew/vessel, secure rigging, establish propulsion

Jury Rigging Essentials

- Improvised rig to safely reach port

Rigging Maintenance Importance

- Regular inspections/preventive replacements drastically reduce risk

By following this clearly formatted checklist, sailors can effectively manage, prevent, and respond to demasting incidents.

CHAPTER 31

ONBOARD FIRES

Fire Prevention Strategies

Fires on boats can be catastrophic, as confined spaces, flammable materials, and limited escape routes create significant risks for everyone on board. Preventing fires on a boat requires meticulous planning, regular maintenance, proper equipment, and education for all passengers and crew.

Understanding Fire Risks on Boats

- Recognize common fire hazards: fuel, oil, propane, and other flammables.
- Check electrical systems for faulty wiring, short circuits, or overloads.
- Exercise caution with cooking equipment (stoves, grills, propane).
- Monitor engine heat and ensure proper ventilation.
- Dispose of smoking materials safely.

Electrical System Safety

   a. Regular Inspections
- Conduct routine checks for frayed wires, loose connections, and corrosion.
- Inspect junction boxes and panels for wear and tear.

   b. Use Marine-Grade Components
- Install only marine-rated wires, connectors, and parts.
- Replace damaged components immediately.

   c. Circuit Protection
- Equip all circuits with the correct fuses or breakers.
- Install GFCIs in wet areas (galley, heads).

   d. Battery Maintenance
- Secure batteries in a ventilated compartment.
- Clean terminals regularly to prevent corrosion.
- Use a battery switch to cut power when not in use.

Fuel System Safety

   a. Inspections and Maintenance
- Regularly examine fuel tanks, lines, and fittings for leaks or corrosion.
- Replace hoses and fittings with marine-approved components.

   b. Refueling Safety
- Turn off engines, electrical systems, and open flames before refueling.
- Avoid overfilling tanks and clean spills immediately.

- ° Ventilate thoroughly after refueling.

c. Fuel Storage

- ° Store portable fuel containers in well-ventilated areas.
- ° Ensure all fuel tanks are properly vented.

Engine Room Fire Prevention

a. Cleanliness

- ° Keep engine room free from oil, debris, and excess fuel.
- ° Clean drip pans and bilge areas regularly.

b. Ventilation

- ° Confirm adequate airflow to prevent overheating or vapor buildup.
- ° Check vents for blockages.

c. Install Fire Suppression

- ° Use an automatic fire suppression system in the engine room.

Galley and Cooking Equipment Safety

a. Marine-Rated Appliances

- ° Use cooking equipment designed for marine use.

b. Propane System Safety

- ° Store tanks in ventilated lockers.
- ° Check lines for leaks before use.
- ° Turn off propane at the tank when not in use.

c. Fire Blankets

- ° Keep a fire blanket in the galley to smother small grease fires.

Fire Detection and Extinguishing Equipment

a. Smoke and Gas Detectors

- ○ Install in sleeping areas, galley, and near engine room.
- ○ Include propane/fuel vapor detectors.

b. Fire Extinguishers

- ○ Place Coast Guard-approved extinguishers in accessible spots (cockpit, galley, engine room, berths).
- ○ Choose appropriate classes (A, B, C) for different fire types.
- ○ Inspect regularly and service or replace as needed.

General Safety Practices

a. No Smoking

- ○ Prohibit smoking near flammable materials.
- ○ Provide safe disposal areas for cigarette butts.

b. Emergency Drills

- ○ Conduct fire drills to practice escape routes and extinguisher use.

c. Proper Ventilation

- ○ Keep enclosed areas ventilated to prevent vapor buildup.

Emergency Preparedness

a. Communication

- ○ Have a working VHF radio and backup handheld radio.

b. Life Jackets and Rafts
- ° Keep enough life jackets on board for everyone.
- ° Carry an emergency life raft for offshore trips.

c. Abandon Ship Plan
- ° Know procedures for launching life rafts and accounting for passengers.

Regular Inspections and Maintenance

a. Pre-Trip Inspections
- ° Check electrical wiring, fuel systems, engine compartment, and firefighting gear.

b. Professional Inspections
- ° Schedule annual inspections to catch issues early.

Using Fire Extinguishers

1. Fire Classifications
- **Class A:** Ordinary combustibles (wood, paper, cloth).
- **Class B:** Flammable liquids (gasoline, oil, grease).
- **Class C:** Electrical equipment (wiring, motors).
- **Class D:** Combustible metals (magnesium, titanium).
- **Class K:** Cooking oils/fats.

2. Types of Fire Extinguishers and Their Uses
- **Water (Class A)**
  - ° Cool burning materials, not for liquids or electrical fires.
- **Foam (Class A, B)**
  - ° Forms a barrier on flammable liquids, not for electrical fires.

- **Carbon Dioxide (Class B, C)**
  - Displaces oxygen, great for electrical fires, leaves no residue.
- **Dry Chemical**
  - **ABC Extinguishers:** Cover A, B, C fires (versatile).
  - **BC Extinguishers:** For flammable liquids and electrical fires only.
- **Wet Chemical (Class K)**
  - For grease/oil fires in kitchens.
- **Specialized (Class D)**
  - For combustible metals only.

3. How to Use a Fire Extinguisher (PASS Method)

- **Pull** the pin.
- **Aim** at the base of the fire.
- **Squeeze** the handle.
- **Sweep** side to side.

4. Choosing the Right Extinguisher

- **Home/Office:** ABC is most versatile.
- **Kitchen:** Wet chemical for grease fires.
- **Workshops:** Class D for metal fires.
- **Boats/Vehicles:** CO_2 or dry chemical for electrical/fuel fires.

5. Maintenance and Inspection

- **Regular Checks:** Ensure correct pressure, no damage, not expired.
- **Refill/Replace:** After any use or if expired.
- **Training:** Show all passengers/crew how to use extinguishers.

EVACUATION PROTOCOLS

1. Immediate Fire Response

- **Raise the Alarm:** Shout "Fire!" and activate alarms/horns.
- **Assess the Fire:** Identify source and severity (engine, galley, fuel).
- **Attempt to Extinguish:** If safe, use correct extinguisher.
- **Cut Off the Source:** Turn off fuel and electrical power if possible.
- Evacuate if the fire cannot be controlled quickly.

2. Notify Authorities

- **VHF Radio Distress Call:** Broadcast MAYDAY on Channel 16.
- **Give Position/Details:** Boat name, location, nature of fire, number on board.
- **EPIRB:** Activate if available for immediate rescue signaling.

3. Assign Roles and Evacuate

- **Captain/Leader:** Direct evacuation, keep order.
- **Firefighter:** Attempt containment if it's still safe.
- **Communication Lead:** Maintain contact with rescue authorities.
- **Passengers:** Move to muster station, don life jackets, follow crew instructions.

4. Prepare to Abandon Ship

- **Launch Life Rafts:** Secure to boat before boarding.

- **Transfer Emergency Supplies:** Bring water, food, first aid, flares.
- **Orderly Boarding:** Help those with mobility issues; keep calm.
- **Cut the Line:** Once everyone is safely aboard and distance from the burning vessel is needed.

5. Survival and Rescue

- **Signal for Help:** Use flares, whistles, EPIRB, and VHF radio.
- **Stay Together:** Remain in or near the raft, conserve energy and supplies.
- **Monitor Burning Vessel:** Watch for explosions or debris.

6. Key Preparations for Fire Evacuation

- **Emergency Drills:** Practice with crew/passengers regularly.
- **Emergency Supplies:** Keep a grab bag with first aid, flashlights, navigation tools, and signaling gear.
- **Functional Communication:** Ensure VHF radio, EPIRB, and backups are in working order.

7. Post-Incident Procedures

- **Report the Incident:** Notify local maritime authorities.
- **Insurance Claims:** File as needed.
- **Review and Improve:** Analyze the incident to strengthen future safety measures.

Chapter 32

MAN OVERBOARD SITUATIONS

QUICK RESPONSE TECHNIQUES

Immediate Actions

Shout "Man Overboard"

- Loudly announce to alert everyone on the boat
- Designate someone to coordinate the rescue effort

Maintain Visual Contact

- Assign a spotter to watch the person in the water
- Continuously point toward the MOB to guide rescuers

Throw Flotation Devices

- Immediately throw a life ring or buoy toward the MOB
- Attach a rescue line or lighted marker if available

Stop the Boat

- Reduce speed and, if safe, turn off the engine
- Engage "man overboard" mode on navigation system to mark position

Maneuver the Boat

Quick Turn Maneuvers

- Williamson Turn: Hard turn one side, reverse helm to circle back
- Figure Eight Turn: Loop around, return on straight path
- Quick Stop (Sailboats): Head into wind to halt forward motion

Approach the MOB

- Approach into the wind/current for better control
- Slow down to prevent waves pushing MOB away

Rescue the Person

Use Rescue Equipment

- Lifelines, rescue ladder, MOB pole—anything to bring MOB closer

Assess Their Condition

- If conscious: Keep calm, guide them aboard
- If unconscious: Use sling or harness to lift safely

Minimize Risk During Retrieval

- Avoid leaning too far overboard
- Use multiple helpers if needed

Post-Rescue Care

Assess for Injuries

- Check for cuts, bruises, shock, hypothermia

Treat Hypothermia

- Remove wet clothing, wrap in dry blankets, offer warm fluids if conscious

Contact Authorities

- Call Coast Guard or rescue services if medical attention needed

Preventing Future Incidents

Safety Equipment

- Require life jackets in rough conditions
- Use harnesses/jacklines for added security

Training and Drills

- Practice MOB scenarios regularly

Secure the Deck

- Stow gear properly, use railings/lifelines

Special Considerations

Rough Seas

- Act quickly—currents and waves move MOB fast

Night Rescues

- Use searchlights, reflective gear, PLBs to track MOB

Multiple People Overboard

- Provide flotation to each, maintain visual contact, call for immediate help

Summary of MOB Protocol

- **Alert and Assign**: Call "Man Overboard," assign roles (spotter, rescuer, driver)
- **Stop and Mark**: Stop boat, mark location, throw flotation devices
- **Maneuver**: Execute appropriate turn to MOB
- **Rescue**: Approach carefully, use rescue gear
- **Post-Rescue**: Check injuries, treat hypothermia, notify authorities

USING RESCUE EQUIPMENT

Personal Safety Gear

Life Jackets (PFDs)

- USCG-approved, whistles, strobe lights, reflective tape

Harnesses and Tethers

- Use with jacklines

Personal Locator Beacons (PLBs)

- Wearable devices transmitting location

Flotation and Retrieval Devices

Lifebuoys (Ring Buoys)

- Immediate flotation, rope/strobe attachments

Throw Bags

- Rope-filled bags for retrieval

Man Overboard Pole (MOB Pole)

- Tall marker with flotation, flag/light

Life Raft or Life sling

- Extra flotation; sling helps retrieval

Retrieval Equipment

Rescue Ladder

- Collapsible/fixed for easy boarding

Rescue Net or Stretcher

- Ideal for unconscious/injured persons

Lifting Harness or Hoist

- Mechanical/manual system for heavier individuals

Search and Recovery Aids

Automatic Identification System (AIS) Beacon

- Transmits MOB position to navigation

EPIRB (Emergency Position Indicating Radio Beacon)

- Alerts authorities with location

Spotlight or Searchlight

- Scanning at night

Signal Flares

- Attract attention for rescue

First Aid and Post-Rescue Gear

First Aid Kit

- Treat injuries, hypothermia, thermal blankets included

Hypothermia Blanket or Bivy Bag

- Retains body heat

Fresh Water and Dry Clothing

- Essential for rehydration, warmth

Navigation and Communication Tools

VHF Radio

- Announce MOB on Channel 16

GPS and MOB Button

- Mark exact location

Whistles and Horns

- Audible signals to alert vessels

Training Equipment

Dummy or Training Manikin

- Practice MOB drills realistically

Instruction Manuals

- Waterproof guides for rescue gear

PREVENTING HYPOTHERMIA

Immediate Actions in Water

Encourage MOB to Stay Calm

- Conserve energy, avoid panic

Use HELP Position

- Cross arms, pull knees up

Group Huddle (Multiple MOBs)

- Share body heat

Avoid Swimming

- Only swim to reach flotation or gear

Minimize Time in Water

Deploy Flotation Devices

- Buoys, rings, rafts

Approach Carefully

- Limit waves pushing MOB away

Use Rescue Equipment

- Quickly bring MOB aboard

Onboard Care After Rescue

Assess Condition

- Shivering, confusion, weak pulse

Remove Wet Clothing

- Prevent further heat loss

Insulate and Warm

- Wrap in blankets, core warming

External Heat Sources

- Warm packs to chest, armpits, groin

Warm Fluids

- Warm water, tea, soup; no alcohol or caffeine

Treating Severe Hypothermia

Handle with Care

- Avoid sudden movements

Avoid Aggressive Rewarming

- Gradual core warming only

Seek Medical Attention

- Contact rescue, provide details

Long-Term Preventive Measures

Wear Appropriate Clothing

- Insulated, waterproof, dry suits

Life Jackets with Thermal Protection

- Extra insulation for cold water

Conduct MOB Drills

- Include hypothermia prevention

Emergency Supplies Onboard

- Thermal blankets, dry clothes, warm beverages

Key Takeaways

- Quick Action: Reduce exposure
- HELP Position: Conserve heat
- Controlled Rewarming: Warm gently
- Preparation: Stock thermal gear, maintain rescue equipment, conduct drills

PART SEVEN

MEDICAL EMERGENCIES

Chapter 33

COMMON INJURIES AND ILLNESSES

Seasickness

Cause: Motion affects the inner ear, leading to conflicting signals about balance.

Risk: Dehydration, inability to perform tasks, and potential vomiting.

Treatment:
- Move to a stable area (center/stern), focus on horizon.
- Use OTC meds (e.g., Dramamine) or prescription patches (Scopolamine).
- Hydrate with small sips of water or ginger ale; rest in fresh air.

Dehydration

Cause: Inadequate fluid intake, excessive heat or sun exposure, vomiting/diarrhea.

Risk: Fatigue, confusion, organ dysfunction in severe cases.

Treatment:

- Increase fluid intake with water or oral rehydration solutions (ORS).
- Cool the person; move to shaded area.
- In severe cases, seek IV fluids and medical attention.

Sunburn

Cause: Overexposure to UV rays without adequate protection (sunscreen, clothing).

Risk: Pain, blistering, heat exhaustion, risk of skin damage or cancer.

Treatment:

- Cool compresses or aloe vera gel to soothe skin.
- Stay out of direct sun; hydrate and use pain relievers (e.g., ibuprofen).
- Cover burned areas and monitor for signs of infection.

Heat Exhaustion

Cause: Prolonged heat exposure and physical exertion leading to excessive sweating.

Risk: Dehydration, dizziness, weakness, can progress to heatstroke.

Treatment:

- Move to a cool, shaded area; have the person lie down.
- Provide cool water or electrolyte drinks; loosen clothing.
- Apply cool compresses; monitor closely for worsening symptoms.

Heatstroke

Cause: Extreme heat exposure without sufficient cooling or hydration.

Risk: Very high body temperature, confusion, potential organ failure.

Treatment:

- Call emergency services immediately.
- Rapidly cool the body (ice packs to neck, groin, armpits).
- Fan the person or douse with cool water; monitor vitals until help arrives.

Hypothermia

Cause: Prolonged exposure to cold water or air, even in moderate climates.

Risk: Shivering, confusion, cardiac arrest in severe cases.

Treatment:

- Move the person to a warm, sheltered area; remove wet clothing.
- Warm the core gradually with blankets or warm packs (chest, neck).
- Provide warm (not hot) fluids if conscious; seek medical attention if severe.

Drowning / Near-Drowning

Cause: Falling overboard, inability to swim, or underwater entrapment.

Risk: Oxygen deprivation, lung damage, potential death.

Treatment:

- Safely remove person from water; check breathing and pulse.
- Begin CPR if no breathing or pulse; use AED if available.
- Keep them warm and seek immediate medical care.

Cuts and Lacerations

Cause: Accidents with fishing gear, tools, or sharp edges on the boat.

Risk: Blood loss, infection, impaired mobility if severe.

Treatment:

- Clean the wound with fresh water or saline; apply pressure to stop bleeding.
- Dress with sterile gauze or bandage; monitor for infection.
- Seek medical help if wound is deep or bleeding is uncontrollable.

Broken Bones (Fractures)

Cause: Falls, slips, heavy objects shifting in rough seas.

Risk: Severe pain, limited mobility, potential complications if not immobilized.

Treatment:

- Stabilize the injured area with a splint or improvised support.
- Apply cold compress to reduce swelling; elevate if possible.

- Seek professional medical care for proper realignment and casting.

Sprains and Strains

Cause: Overextension or twisting of joints during sudden boat movement.

Risk: Pain, swelling, reduced function.

Treatment:

- Follow R.I.C.E. (Rest, Ice, Compression, Elevation).
- Use elastic bandage for support; avoid weight-bearing if painful.
- Gradually return to activity once pain/ swelling subsides.

Burns

Cause: Contact with hot surfaces (engine parts, stoves) or boiling liquids.

Risk: Pain, blistering, infection, scarring.

Treatment:

- Cool the burn under running water for several minutes.
- Cover with sterile, non-stick dressing; do not pop blisters.
- Seek professional care for severe or extensive burns.

Jellyfish or Marine Animal Stings

Cause: Contact with jellyfish tentacles, stingrays, or other marine animals.

Risk: Pain, swelling, possible allergic reactions or secondary infection.

Treatment:

- Rinse with salt water (not fresh water); remove visible tentacles carefully.
- Soak in hot water (if stingray or certain jellyfish) or use vinegar for some jellyfish.
- Monitor for allergic reactions; seek medical help for severe symptoms.

Fishhook Injuries

Cause: Accidental embedding of hooks in skin while fishing or handling gear.

Risk: Pain, tissue damage, infection if not cleaned.

Treatment:

- If possible, push hook forward to remove barb or use a "back-out" technique.
- Clean thoroughly with antiseptic, dress with sterile bandage.
- Seek medical help if deep or near sensitive areas (eyes, joints).

Allergic Reactions

Cause: Allergies to food, insect stings, or marine life (e.g., shellfish).

Risk: Itching, swelling, hives, possible anaphylaxis (life-threatening).

Treatment:

- Administer oral antihistamines for mild reactions.
- Use an epinephrine auto-injector (EpiPen) for severe symptoms.
- Seek emergency care if breathing difficulty or facial swelling occurs.

Cardiac Arrest

Cause: Heart attack, severe heart conditions exacerbated by stress or exertion.

Risk: Sudden loss of consciousness, requires immediate intervention.

Treatment:

- Call for help (Mayday if at sea); begin CPR immediately.
- Use an AED if available; follow voice prompts.
- Continue until the person revives or professional help arrives.

Respiratory Distress

Cause: Asthma, smoke inhalation, or severe allergic reactions.

Risk: Difficulty breathing, low oxygen, can lead to unconsciousness.

Treatment:

- Move person to fresh air; sit them upright.
- Use rescue inhaler (if prescribed); administer oxygen if available.
- Call for immediate medical assistance if breathing worsens.

Shock

Cause: Severe injury, blood loss, extreme emotional distress.

Risk: Pale, clammy skin, weak pulse, possible organ failure.

Treatment:

- Lay the person flat, elevate legs (if no injury to head/neck/spine).
- Keep them warm; reassure and monitor vitals.
- Stop any bleeding; seek immediate medical care.

Head Injuries

Cause: Falls, impact with hard surfaces, or thrown objects on deck.

Risk: Concussion, confusion, severe brain injury.

Treatment:

- Immobilize head/neck if severe; monitor for loss of consciousness.
- Apply cold pack if swelling; keep person awake to observe symptoms.
- Seek medical attention for severe headache, vomiting, or confusion.

Infections

Cause: Cuts, scrapes, or wounds exposed to saltwater, poor hygiene.

Risk: Swelling, redness, fever, potential serious complications if untreated.

Treatment:

- Clean wound thoroughly, apply antibiotic ointment.

- Change dressings regularly; watch for increased redness or pus.
- Seek medical care if signs of severe infection or fever.

Diabetic Emergencies

Cause: Low (hypoglycemia) or high (hyperglycemia) blood sugar levels.

Risk: Dizziness, confusion, loss of consciousness, coma if untreated.

Treatment:

- If low blood sugar: Provide fast-acting sugar (glucose tabs, juice).
- If high blood sugar: Encourage hydration and, if possible, administer insulin as prescribed.
- Seek immediate medical help if condition doesn't improve or worsens.

PREVENTION, DIAGNOSIS AND TREATMENT OF COMMON MEDICAL EMERGENCIES

Seasickness

Seasickness, a form of motion sickness, occurs when the brain receives conflicting signals from the inner ear, eyes, and body about motion and balance. While it's not life-threatening, it can severely impact the enjoyment and functionality of individuals on a boat. Below is a detailed guide on preventing, diagnosing, and treating seasickness.

Prevention of Seasickness

Behavioral and Environmental Strategies

1. Choose a Stable Position on the Boat:

- Stay in the center of the boat or near the stern, where movement is least pronounced.

- Face forward and look at the horizon to maintain a stable reference point.

2. Avoid Triggers:

- Refrain from reading or staring at objects inside the boat while moving.
- Avoid strong odors (e.g., diesel fumes or strong food smells).

3. Stay Hydrated and Eat Light:

- Consume light, non-greasy meals before boarding (e.g., crackers or bananas).
- Avoid heavy, spicy, or acidic foods and alcohol before and during the trip.

4. Get Fresh Air:

- Spend time on the deck where there is good ventilation.
- Avoid enclosed, poorly ventilated areas of the boat.

5. Minimize Head Movement:

- Keep your head steady and avoid sudden, jerky movements.

6. Acclimate Before the Trip:

- Spend time on a docked boat or take short trips to get used to the motion.

Medication for Prevention

Over-the-Counter Medications:

- **Dimenhydrinate (Dramamine)** or **Meclizine (Bonine)**:
  - Take 1-2 hours before boarding.

- ◦ Reduces nausea and dizziness by blocking motion-related signals in the brain.
- Side Effects: Drowsiness and dry mouth.

Prescription Medications:

- **Scopolamine (Transdermal Patch)**:
  - ◦ Apply behind the ear at least 4 hours before travel.
  - ◦ Provides long-lasting relief (up to 72 hours).
- Side Effects: Dry mouth, dizziness, and blurred vision.

Natural Remedies:

- **Ginger**:
  - ◦ Consume ginger tea, candies, or supplements to reduce nausea.
- **Peppermint**:
  - ◦ Sucking on peppermint lozenges or using peppermint oil may help.

Acupressure Bands:

- Wear wristbands designed to stimulate pressure points (e.g., the **P14 point** on the inner wrist)

Diagnosis of Seasickness

Seasickness is diagnosed based on symptoms and exposure to motion. The condition manifests differently in individuals, but common signs include:

Early Symptoms

- Nausea or queasiness.
- Dizziness or lightheadedness.
- Cold sweats.

Progressive Symptoms

- Vomiting.
- Fatigue or weakness.
- Pale skin.
- Difficulty concentrating or irritability.

Key Diagnostic Feature

- Symptoms typically resolve once motion stops, though some people experience lingering effects for hours.

Treatment of Seasickness

Once seasickness begins, the goal is to manage symptoms and provide comfort. Use a combination of strategies:

Immediate Interventions

1. Change Position:

- Move to a stable area on the boat (center or stern).
- Face forward and focus on the horizon.

2. Lie Down:

- Lie flat on your back with your eyes closed to reduce conflicting signals.

3. Cool the Body:

- Apply a cold compress to the forehead or neck to alleviate nausea.
- Wear loose, comfortable clothing to avoid overheating.

4. Hydrate:

- Sip water, ginger ale, or clear fluids to prevent dehydration.

- Avoid large gulps, which may worsen nausea.

5. Sniff Fresh Air:

- Open a window or step onto the deck for fresh air.

Symptomatic Relief with Medications

1. Immediate Use of OTC Medications:

- Take **Dimenhydrinate (Dramamine)** or **Meclizine (Bonine)** for fast symptom relief.
- Use chewable tablets if swallowing pills is difficult.

2. Prescription Medications:

- For severe cases, consider **Scopolamine**, but consult a medical professional for guidance.

3. Anti-Nausea Remedies:

- Suck on ginger candies or drink ginger tea to alleviate nausea.
- Use peppermint essential oil to inhale or massage lightly on the temples.

Supportive Care

1. Encourage Rest:

- Allow the affected person to rest in a calm, quiet environment.

2. Small Snacks:

- Offer bland snacks like crackers to settle the stomach.

3. Monitor for Dehydration:

- Watch for signs such as dry lips, decreased urination, or dark-colored urine.

Long-Term Management

For those prone to seasickness, implement these measures for future trips:

1. Conditioning:

- Gradually expose yourself to boat travel to build tolerance.

2. Dietary Adjustments:

- Maintain a light, low-fat diet before and during boating trips.

3. Pre-Medication:

- Take preventive medication or wear acupressure bands before symptoms develop.

4. Boat Selection:

- Opt for larger, more stable boats if possible, as they cause less motion.

When to Seek Medical Attention

Although rare, severe cases of seasickness may require professional medical evaluation. Contact a doctor if:

- Vomiting persists for several hours.
- Dehydration symptoms become severe (e.g., confusion, rapid heart rate).

- Symptoms do not improve after the motion stops.

By combining prevention, timely intervention, and supportive care, seasickness can be effectively managed, allowing individuals to enjoy their time on the water.

Dehydration

Prevention, Diagnosis, and Treatment of Severe Dehydration

Severe dehydration occurs when the body loses more fluids than it takes in, leading to significant physiological disturbances. This condition can be life-threatening, especially in remote or resource-limited settings, such as on a boat or during extended outdoor activities. Below is a detailed guide to preventing, diagnosing, and treating severe dehydration.

Prevention of Severe Dehydration

Hydration Strategies

1. Regular Fluid Intake:
- Drink water frequently, even if you're not thirsty, especially in hot or physically demanding conditions.
- Aim for at least 2–3 liters (8–12 cups) of water per day, more if sweating heavily.

2. Electrolyte Balance:
- Consume drinks with electrolytes, like oral rehydration solutions (ORS), sports drinks, or coconut water, to

replenish sodium, potassium, and other minerals.
- Include salt in your diet to help retain fluids.

3. Monitor Urine Output:

- Check the color of urine:
  ○ Light yellow = hydrated.
  ○ Dark yellow or amber = dehydrated.

4. Adjust for Conditions:

- In hot, humid weather or during intense physical activity, increase fluid intake.
- Avoid alcohol and caffeine, which can exacerbate dehydration.

5. Eat Hydrating Foods:

- Include fruits and vegetables with high water content, such as watermelon, cucumber, oranges, and lettuce.

Behavioral Strategies

1. Protect Against Heat:

- Wear light, loose clothing and stay in shaded or cool areas when possible.
- Use a wide-brimmed hat or umbrella to reduce sun exposure.

2. Plan Ahead:

- Carry extra water on trips or outdoor activities, especially in remote areas or during extended boat trips.
- Use hydration packs or portable water purification systems in emergency scenarios.

Diagnosis of Severe Dehydration

a. Recognizing Early Symptoms
1. **Thirst and Dryness**:
   - Intense thirst.
   - Dry mouth, throat, and lips.
   - Decreased sweating.
2. **Dark Urine**:
   - Low urine output or very dark-colored urine.

b. Severe Symptoms
1. **Neurological**:
   - Confusion, dizziness, or disorientation.
   - Severe fatigue or lethargy.
   - Irritability or inability to concentrate.
2. **Physical**:
   - Rapid heartbeat and breathing.
   - Sunken eyes or cheeks.
   - Cool, clammy skin or dry, hot skin (in heatstroke).
   - Loss of skin elasticity (pinched skin takes longer to return to normal).
c. **Critical Signs:**
   - Little to no urination for 12 hours or more.
   - Blood pressure drops when standing (postural hypotension).
   - Fainting or unconsciousness.

c. Diagnostic Tools
- **Capillary Refill Test**:
  - Press on the nail bed until it turns white, then release. If it takes longer than 2 seconds for color to return, dehydration may be severe.

- **Body Weight Loss**:
    - ◦ A sudden drop in body weight (more than 13% of body weight) is a sign of significant fluid loss.

Treatment of Severe Dehydration

a. Immediate First Aid

1. **Rehydrate Gradually**:
    - ◦ Provide small sips of water or oral rehydration solution (ORS) if the person is conscious.
    - ◦ Avoid large amounts of water at once, as it may cause nausea or vomiting.

2. **Use ORS**:
    - ◦ Mix ORS (commercial packets or homemade) in clean water:
        - • **Homemade ORS Recipe**: Mix 1 liter of clean water with 14 teaspoons of sugar and 1/2 teaspoon of salt.
    - ◦ ORS helps restore electrolytes and fluids more effectively than plain water.

3. **Cool the Body**:
    - ◦ Move the person to a shaded or cool area.
    - ◦ Apply a damp cloth to the skin or use a fan to lower body temperature.

4. **Monitor Vital Signs**:
    - ◦ Check for pulse, breathing, and responsiveness.
    - ◦ If the person becomes unconscious or their condition worsens, prepare for emergency evacuation.

b. Severe Cases

1. **IV Fluids**:
   - ° In cases of severe dehydration, intravenous (IV) fluids are required to rapidly replenish fluids and electrolytes.
   - ° Administer lactated Ringer's solution or normal saline, if available, under medical supervision.

2. **Hospitalization**:
   - ° Severe dehydration may require hospitalization for continuous monitoring and fluid administration.
   - ° Blood tests may be performed to check electrolyte levels and kidney function.

c. What to Avoid

1. **Caffeinated or Sugary Drinks**:
   - ° Avoid sodas, energy drinks, and coffee, as these can worsen dehydration.

2. **Rapid Fluid Intake**:
   - ° Do not allow the person to drink large quantities of water in a short time, as this can lead to water intoxication (hyponatremia).

Post-Treatment Recovery

1. Gradual Rehydration:

- Continue oral rehydration over several hours or days until urine output and color return to normal.
- Monitor energy levels and physical symptoms.

2. Dietary Adjustments:

- Introduce small, easily digestible meals with a focus on hydrating foods and electrolyte-rich items.

3. Rest and Monitoring:

- Allow the individual to rest and recover fully before resuming normal activities.
- Keep monitoring for any lingering symptoms such as fatigue or confusion.

Prevention of Recurrence

- Educate the individual about the importance of staying hydrated.
- Develop a hydration plan for future activities or trips.
- Ensure access to clean water or water purification tools in remote areas.

Key Takeaways

- **Prevention**: Regular hydration, electrolyte replenishment, and environmental precautions are crucial.
- **Diagnosis**: Recognize early and severe symptoms, such as extreme thirst, confusion, and rapid heartbeat.
- **Treatment**: Administer ORS or IV fluids promptly, cool the body, and avoid overloading with plain water.

By combining prevention strategies with prompt diagnosis and effective treatment, severe dehydration can be managed effectively, even in challenging conditions. if you'd like a detailed guide on preparing ORS or hydration plans!

Sunburn

Definition

- Overexposure to UV (ultraviolet) radiation, causing damage to the skin's outer layers.
- Ranges from mild redness to severe blistering; increases risk of skin cancer over time.

Prevention of Sunburn

Wear Sunscreen

- Use broad-spectrum SPF 30+; apply 20–30 minutes before sun exposure.
- Reapply every 2 hours, or more often if swimming/sweating.

Protective Clothing

- Tightly woven, lightweight, long-sleeved shirts and pants (preferably UPF-rated).

Hats and Sunglasses

- Wide-brimmed hats to shade face, neck, and ears.
- Sunglasses with 100% UV protection.

Seek Shade

- Avoid direct sun 10 AM–4 PM (peak UV hours).
- Use umbrellas, canopies, or other shade structures.

Mind Reflective Surfaces

- Water, sand, and snow reflect UV rays. Take extra precautions in these environments.

Check UV Index

- Monitor local reports; adjust outdoor activities when UV levels are high.

Diagnosis of Sunburn

Mild Sunburn (First-Degree)

- Red, warm skin; mild pain or tenderness.
- Slight swelling possible.

Moderate Sunburn (Second-Degree)

- Red, swollen skin with small blisters.
- More intense pain; peeling skin within days.

Severe Sunburn

- Deep redness or purple discoloration, large/ painful blisters.
- Possible fever, chills, nausea, headache (signs of "sun poisoning").

Risk Factors

- Fair skin, light eyes/hair, children, and older adults are especially vulnerable.
- Severe sunburn can lead to dehydration, heatstroke, or infections (if blisters break).

Treatment of Sunburn

Immediate Care

- Move out of direct sunlight; find shade or go indoors.
- Cool the skin with a damp towel or a cool (not cold) shower/bath.

Relieve Pain and Swelling

- For adults, aspirin (highly effective) or ibuprofen/acetaminophen can reduce pain/inflammation.
- Apply topical corticosteroid ointments at least twice daily until pain/swelling subside.
- Use aloe vera gel or moisturizers without alcohol to soothe skin.

Hydrate

- Drink plenty of water to prevent dehydration and aid recovery.

Protect the Skin

- Avoid popping blisters; cover large or broken blisters with sterile gauze.
- Moisturize gently to support healing and reduce peeling.

Severe Cases

- Watch for fever, chills, nausea (possible sun poisoning). Seek medical attention.
- If blisters become infected (redness, pus), consult a healthcare professional.

Long-Term Recovery and Prevention of Recurrence

Healing Timeline

- Mild sunburn: ~3–7 days.
- Moderate to severe: ~2–3 weeks.

Daily Sunscreen Use

- Apply sunscreen even on cloudy days; keep burned skin covered until healed.

Skin Monitoring

- Watch for changes in moles/freckles; schedule regular skin checks if prone to burns.

Heat Exhaustion

Definition

- Heat-related illness from prolonged heat exposure, heavy sweating, and/or dehydration.
- Can progress to heatstroke if untreated.

Prevention of Heat Exhaustion

Stay Hydrated

- Drink 8–12 cups water/day in normal conditions; more in hot or high-exertion environments.
- Replace electrolytes (sports drinks, ORS) to counter sweat losses.

Regulate Activities

- Avoid strenuous tasks during 10 AM–4 PM (peak heat).
- Take frequent breaks (10–15 mins every hour) in shade or cool areas.

Dress Appropriately

- Wear light-colored, loose-fitting clothing; wide-brimmed hats.
- Use cooling towels or neck wraps.

Environmental Adjustments

- Use fans, AC, or canopies for cooling.

- Acclimate over 7–12 days for better heat tolerance.

Diagnosis of Heat Exhaustion

Early Symptoms
- Heavy sweating, weakness, muscle cramps, nausea/vomiting.
- Dizziness, lightheadedness, or mild confusion.
- Skin is cool, pale, and clammy.

Advanced Symptoms
- Rapid, weak pulse and low blood pressure.
- Rapid breathing; possible fainting spells.

Differentiate from Heatstroke
- Heat Exhaustion: Core temp < 104°F, sweating present, milder mental changes.
- Heatstroke: Core temp > 104°F, often no sweating, severe confusion/unconsciousness.

Treatment of Heat Exhaustion

Immediate First Aid
- Move to a shaded/AC area; lie down, elevate legs.
- Rehydrate with cool water or electrolyte fluids (small sips).
- Cool the body (wet towels, ice packs at neck/armpits/groin, fanning).

Monitor Symptoms
- Check every 10–15 mins for improvement (reduced dizziness, better skin color).

- Seek medical help if no improvement after ~30 mins or if condition worsens.

Severe Cases

- IV fluids may be needed.
- Continuous monitoring of vital signs in a clinical setting.

Recovery and Follow-Up

Rest and Rehydrate

- Avoid strenuous activity for 24–48 hours; replenish fluids thoroughly.

Address Contributing Factors

- Reduce heat exposure next time, adjust workload/breaks.

Gradual Return

- Reintroduce physical tasks slowly while watching for any early symptoms.

Heatstroke

Definition

- A life-threatening heat-related condition where the body's cooling mechanisms fail.
- Characterized by a core body temperature > 104°F (40°C).

Comparison with Heat Exhaustion

Heat Exhaustion
- Body temp < 104°F, profuse sweating, milder confusion.

Heatstroke
- Body temp > 104°F, often cessation of sweating, severe confusion or unconsciousness, risk of organ failure.

Prevention of Heatstroke
(Same core strategies as Heat Exhaustion, but with heightened caution.)

Diagnosis of Heatstroke

Key Indicators
- Very high body temperature (above 104°F).
- Hot, dry, or flushed skin (sweating may stop).
- Rapid, strong pulse; possible seizures, unconsciousness.

Treatment of Heatstroke

Call Emergency Services Immediately
- This is a medical emergency; dial 911 (or local equivalent).

Aggressive Cooling
- Apply ice packs to neck, armpits, groin; douse with cool water if possible.
- Use fans or air conditioning to accelerate cooling.

Avoid Oral Fluids if Unconscious

- IV fluids needed in a clinical setting.

Monitor Vital Signs

- Watch for shock, seizures, or cardiac arrhythmias.

Key Takeaways

Heatstroke requires **immediate** hospitalization. Without rapid intervention, there is a high risk of organ damage or death.

Hypothermia

Definition

- Body core temperature drops below 95°F (35°C).
- Can result from cold water exposure, cold air, or prolonged wet conditions.

Prevention of Hypothermia

Proper Clothing

- Layering: Moisture-wicking base, insulating mid-layer, waterproof/windproof outer layer.
- Hat, gloves, warm socks, waterproof footwear.

Environmental/Behavioral Strategies

- Stay dry—wet clothing accelerates heat loss.
- Limit exposure to cold/wind; use windbreaks or shelters.
- Carry emergency thermal blankets, extra clothes, and fire-starting materials.

Hydration and Nutrition

- Drink warm, non-alcoholic fluids; eat high-energy foods for heat production.

Plan Ahead

- Monitor weather; avoid extreme conditions if possible.
- Gradual acclimatization to cold environments.

Diagnosis of Hypothermia

Mild Hypothermia (90–95°F / 32–35°C)

- Shivering, cold/pale skin, fatigue, rapid breathing/heart rate.
- Slight confusion, reduced coordination.

Moderate Hypothermia (82–90°F / 28–32°C)

- Shivering may stop, slurred speech, pronounced confusion.
- Slow pulse/breathing, stumbling, loss of fine motor skills.

Severe Hypothermia (<82°F / <28°C)

- Possible unconsciousness, very slow/absent pulse, stiff muscles.
- Risk of cardiac arrest.

Treatment of Hypothermia

Mild Hypothermia

- Move to a warm shelter, remove wet clothing.
- Wrap in blankets/sleeping bags, offer warm (not hot) sweet fluids.

- Passive rewarming (body heat, insulation).

Moderate Hypothermia

- Active external rewarming: Warm compresses or heating pads on neck, chest, armpits, groin.
- Handle gently; monitor for irregular breathing/ heart rate.

Severe Hypothermia

- Call emergency services; requires hospital-based rewarming (warm IV fluids, heated oxygen).
- Do not assume death; the heart may be very slow but still viable.
- Avoid sudden movements or rewarming extremities first (risk of "afterdrop").

Recovery and Long-Term Management

Rest and Rehabilitation

- Allow the body to recover; address any frostbite or respiratory issues.

Prevent Future Incidents

- Proper gear, planning, and vigilance against moisture/cold.

Monitor for Complications

- Watch for arrhythmias, shock, or infection in severe cases.
- Reasoned for 17 seconds

Drowning/Near Drowning

Definition

- Drowning: Water submersion causing respiratory impairment, potentially leading to death.
- Near-Drowning: Survival after water immersion, but with risk of complications (e.g., secondary drowning).

Prevention of Drowning

Safe Swimming Practices

- Supervise children/inexperienced swimmers; designate a "water watcher."
- Learn to swim; practice floating/treading water.
- Avoid alcohol when swimming/boating.
- Swim in designated areas with lifeguards; avoid strong currents.

Boating and Water Sports Safety

- Wear Coast Guard-approved life jackets (properly fitted).
- Check water conditions (tides, currents, weather).
- Equip boats with emergency flotation; avoid overloading.

Home and Pool Safety

- Install four-sided pool fencing, self-closing/latching gates.
- Keep life rings, reaching poles, and a phone near pools.
- Remove toys/floats from the water to prevent unsupervised entry.

Diagnosis of Drowning/Near-Drowning

Recognizing Drowning

- Active: Silent struggle, head tilted back, arms flailing, mouth at water level.
- Passive: Person found face-down, motionless, or unconscious.

Symptoms of Near Drowning

- Immediate: Coughing, breathing difficulty, frothy sputum, cyanosis, confusion.
- Delayed (Secondary Drowning): Breathing problems, chest pain, persistent cough, fatigue hours later.

Treatment of Drowning/Near-Drowning

Immediate Rescue

- Call for help; notify emergency services.
- Use reaching/throwing devices (rope, life ring).
- Only enter water if trained and safe to do so.

Initial First Aid

- Check responsiveness; if unresponsive, start CPR immediately.
- Adults CPR: 30 compressions, 2 breaths.
- Children/Infants CPR: 15 compressions, 2 breaths if trained in pediatric CPR.
- Clear airway gently if obstructed; watch for vomiting.

Oxygen & Advanced Care

- Administer 100% oxygen if available.
- Transport to hospital for evaluation (risk of secondary drowning).

- Possible chest X-rays, blood tests, or mechanical ventilation in severe cases.

Key Takeaways

- **Prevention:** Supervision, life jackets, safe swimming practices.
- **Diagnosis:** Recognize drowning signs, watch for delayed symptoms in near-drowning.
- **Treatment:** Immediate rescue, CPR, medical follow-up for all near-drowning events.

Cuts and Lacerations

Definition

- Open wounds caused by sharp objects, fishing gear, or accidental falls.
- High risk of infection at sea due to marine bacteria and limited medical access.

Immediate Response

Stop the Bleeding

- Apply direct pressure with clean cloth/gauze.
- Elevate injury above heart level if possible.
- Use a tourniquet only for life-threatening bleeding; note application time.

Clean the Wound

Rinse Thoroughly
- Use bottled/distilled water or saline solution.
- Avoid seawater (bacterial contamination).
- Remove debris with sterile tweezers if superficial.

Disinfect
- Apply antiseptics like hydrogen peroxide or povidone-iodine.
- Clean gently to avoid damaging healthy tissue.

Close the Wound (If Necessary)

Small Cuts
- May be left open to air if not bleeding significantly.

Large/Deep Lacerations
- Use sterile adhesive strips (e.g., Steri-Strips) or butterfly bandages to approximate edges.
- If trained, use temporary sutures/staples for gaping wounds until professional care is available.

Bandage the Wound

Sterile Dressing
- Cover with sterile gauze; secure with tape or bandage.

Waterproof Covering
- Use waterproof bandages if the wound may get wet.

Pain Management

Medications
- Ibuprofen or acetaminophen for pain and swelling.

Cold Compress
- Apply ice packs for 15–20 minutes to reduce inflammation.

Monitor for Infection

Signs of Infection
- Redness, swelling, warmth, pus, fever.

Infection Management
- Re-clean and re-dress daily.
- Use topical antibiotics or oral antibiotics if symptoms worsen.

Special Considerations

Deep Wounds
- Possible tendon/muscle involvement—immobilize and seek help.

Marine-Related Injuries
- Rinse with clean water; apply vinegar if stung by certain marine life.

Embedded Objects
- Stabilize but do not remove deeply embedded objects; seek professional care.

When to Seek Medical Attention

Immediate Care

- Deep, gaping wounds or uncontrollable bleeding.
- Involvement of joints, tendons, or sensitive areas.
- Signs of severe infection or no healing progress within 48 hours.

Emergency Supplies for Wound Care at Sea

Must-Have Items

- Sterile gauze, antiseptic solution, sterile tweezers, adhesive strips, suture kit (if trained), waterproof tape, gloves.

Summary

- **Stop Bleeding, Clean Thoroughly, Close/ Protect, Monitor Infection, Seek Medical Help** when needed.

CHAPTER 35

FRACTURES

Definition

- A break in the bone that can vary from a hairline crack to multiple fragments.
- Severity depends on type (closed, open, displaced, comminuted) and location (extremities, trunk, spine, etc.).

Prevention of Fractures

General Safety

- Keep walking surfaces dry/clear, use non-slip footwear.
- Use protective gear (helmets, padding) for high-risk activities.
- Secure loose objects on boats.

Bone Strength

- Adequate calcium, vitamin D intake.
- Weight-bearing exercises to boost bone density.
- Avoid smoking/excess alcohol.

Diagnosis of Fractures

Common Signs

- Severe pain, swelling, bruising.
- Deformity or limited range of motion.
- Possible "grating" sensation (crepitus).

Types of Fractures

- Closed vs. Open (bone piercing skin).
- Displaced (misaligned) vs. Non-displaced.
- Comminuted (shattered) vs. Hairline.

Treatment by Region

Trunk (Ribs, Pelvis)

- Rib Fractures: Wrap loosely; monitor for breathing complications (pneumothorax).
- Pelvic Fractures: Immobilize with a pelvic binder; high risk of internal bleeding.

Extremities (Arms, Legs, Hands, Feet)

- Arm/Hand: Splint or sling; elevate to reduce swelling; apply ice.
- Leg/Foot: Splint with rigid materials; avoid weight-bearing; elevate and cool.

Head/Neck

- Skull Fracture: Immobilize neck/head; watch for neurological signs.
- Neck Fracture: Cervical collar or rolled towels; do not move unless necessary.

Spine (Vertebrae)

- Keep the person flat on a rigid surface.
- Stabilize neck/spine; avoid movement.

General Principles for All Fractures

Immobilization

- Splint joints above and below fracture.
- Use boards, rolled towels, or commercial splints.

Control Bleeding (Open Fractures)

- Cover wound with sterile dressing; do not push bone back in.
- Manage shock if present.

Pain Management

- OTC pain relievers (ibuprofen, acetaminophen).
- Ice packs (wrapped in cloth) to reduce swelling.

Seek Professional Care

- Open fractures, major deformities, head/neck/spine involvement, or compromised circulation require immediate medical attention.

Key Takeaways

- **Prevent** falls/injuries, **Diagnose** by signs (pain, swelling, deformity), **Treat** by immobilizing and managing pain, then **Seek Medical Help** promptly.

CHAPTER 36

SPRAINS AND STRAINS

Definition

- **Sprain:** Overstretching or tearing ligaments (bone-to-bone).
- **Strain:** Overstretching or tearing muscles/tendons (muscle-to-bone).

Prevention of Sprains and Strains

Strength & Conditioning

- Strengthen muscles around joints (weightlifting, resistance bands).
- Maintain flexibility with regular stretching.
- Develop core stability to enhance balance.

Proper Techniques & Gear

- Warm up (5–10 mins) before activities; cool down after.
- Use safe lifting methods (bend knees, straight back).
- Wear supportive footwear; use braces if needed.

Lifestyle Factors

- Maintain healthy weight to reduce stress on joints.
- Balanced diet (protein, vitamins, minerals).
- Stay hydrated for muscle/tissue health.

Diagnosis of Sprains and Strains

Sprain Severity

- Grade I: Mild ligament stretch, slight pain/swelling.
- Grade II: Partial ligament tear, moderate pain/bruising, some instability.
- Grade III: Complete tear, severe pain/swelling, joint instability.

Strain Severity

- Grade I: Mild overstretching of muscle/tendon, minimal swelling.
- Grade II: Partial tear, more pronounced pain/loss of strength.
- Grade III: Complete tear, severe pain, significant loss of function.

Examination and Diagnostic Tools

Physical Examination

- Check for tenderness, swelling, and any limitations in range of motion.
- Look for instability or deformity in joints indicating a severe sprain/strain.

Imaging Studies

- **X-rays:** Rule out fractures or dislocations.
- **MRI / Ultrasound:** Identify ligament/tendon tears or muscle damage.

Functional Tests

- Controlled movements to assess strength and stability, only if safe to perform.

Treatment of Sprains and Strains

Immediate Care (R.I.C.E. Method)

1. Rest

- Avoid stressing the injured area; use crutches/braces if needed.

2. Ice

- Cold pack wrapped in a cloth for 15–20 minutes every 1–2 hours (first 48–72 hrs).

3. Compression

- Elastic bandage or wrap to reduce swelling and support.

4. Elevation

- Keep injured area above heart level to minimize swelling.

Pain and Inflammation Management

- Over-the-counter pain relievers (e.g., ibuprofen, acetaminophen).

- Short-term use of NSAIDs (avoid prolonged use to not hinder healing).
- Topical anti-inflammatory gels/creams (e.g., diclofenac).

Rehabilitation

1. Range of Motion Exercises

- Gentle stretching once acute swelling subsides.

2. Strengthening Exercises

- Gradually introduce resistance to rebuild muscle and joint support.

3. Proprioception Training

- Balance exercises (single-leg stands, balance boards) to prevent reinjury.

Severe Cases (Grade III)

Complete Muscle/Tendon Rupture:

Intense pain, swelling, inability to use the affected muscle.

1. Immobilization

- Brace, splint, or cast for several weeks if ligaments/ tendons are fully torn.

2. Surgical Repair

- May be needed for complete ligament/tendon tears (e.g., ACL, Achilles).

3. Physical Therapy

- Essential after surgery or long immobilization to restore full function.

Complications to Watch For

Chronic Instability

- Repeated sprains weaken ligaments, leading to ongoing joint issues.

Muscle Atrophy

- Prolonged immobilization can cause significant loss of muscle mass.

Adhesions or Stiffness

- Insufficient rehabilitation may reduce range of motion permanently.

Long-Term Recovery

Gradual Return to Activity

- Avoid rushing back to high-impact sports until fully healed.

Preventive Measures

- Use braces/taping for previously injured areas if needed.

Key Takeaways

- **Prevention:** Strength, flexibility, proper techniques.

- **Diagnosis:** Differentiate severity (Grades I–III) by level of pain, swelling, function loss.
- **Treatment:** Immediate R.I.C.E., possible immobilization or surgery if severe.
- **Outcome:** Most recover fully with correct management and rehab.

Chapter 37

BURNS

Definition and Causes

- Tissue damage from thermal, chemical, electrical, radiation, or friction sources.
- On boats: hot engine parts, scalding water, fuel-related fires.
- On land: house fires, hot liquids, chemicals, electrical wires.

Prevention of Burns

Thermal Burns

- Use heat-resistant gloves, secure hot liquids (boat).
- Keep flammables away from open flames (land).

Chemical Burns

- Label and store chemicals properly.
- Follow safety instructions for corrosive substances.

Electrical Burns

- Inspect wiring, avoid water near electrical systems.
- Replace frayed cords, don't overload circuits.

Radiation Burns

- Sunscreen, hats, UV-protective clothing.
- Limit sun exposure (10 AM–4 PM).

Friction Burns

- Wear gloves (boat lines), avoid dragging skin on rough surfaces.

Diagnosis of Burns

First-Degree (Superficial)

- Red, mild swelling, no blisters.
- Typically from brief contact with hot objects or mild sunburn.

Second-Degree (Partial-Thickness)

- Red, blistered, intense pain, possible weeping.
- Caused by scalds, longer contact with hot surfaces.

Third-Degree (Full-Thickness)

- Charred or white, leathery skin.
- May be painless if nerves are destroyed.

Treatment of Burns

First-Degree

- Cool with running water (10–20 mins).

- Apply aloe vera or mild burn ointment; cover with non-stick dressing.

Second-Degree

- Cool with water, don't break blisters.
- Use antibiotic cream, sterile non-stick dressing; watch for infection.

Third-Degree

- **Do not** apply water if extensive; risk of shock.
- Cover with clean, dry cloth; seek immediate medical care.

Specialized Situations

Chemical Burns

- Flush with water ≥20 mins, remove contaminated clothing.
- Cover with sterile dressing; get professional help.

Electrical Burns

- Turn off power source first; check breathing and pulse.
- Look for entry/exit wounds; may have internal damage.

Radiation (Severe Sunburn)

- Cool with damp cloth, apply aloe vera/hydrocortisone.
- Prevent further exposure; consult doctor if severe.

Friction Burns

- Clean gently with soap/water, apply antibiotic ointment.
- Cover with non-stick dressing; change daily.

Monitoring and Complications

Signs of Infection
- Increased redness, swelling, pus, fever.

Long-Term Care
- Severe burns: possible skin grafts, rehab, scar management.
- Use scar-reducing creams or silicone sheets if needed.

Key Takeaways

- **Prevention:** Proper handling of heat sources, chemicals, electricity, sun protection.
- **Diagnosis:** Classify burn depth (1st, 2nd, 3rd) and size.
- **Treatment:** Cool water for minor burns, cover, watch for infection; emergency care for major burns.

CHAPTER 38

MARINE ANIMAL STINGS

Definition

- Stings from jellyfish, stingrays, sea urchins, or other venomous marine life.
- Can range from mild irritation to life-threatening reactions.

Prevention of Marine Animal Stings

Awareness and Avoidance

- Research local marine hazards; heed warnings about jellyfish blooms.
- Avoid swimming in high-risk zones; do not touch marine creatures.

Protective Gear

- Wear wetsuits, rash guards, water shoes.
- Shuffle feet in shallow water to avoid stingrays.

Diagnosis of Stings

Jellyfish

- Immediate pain/burning, red welts, possible severe systemic reactions.

Stingray

- Barb puncture with intense local pain, swelling, possible infection risk.

Sea Urchin

- Sharp spines causing punctures, localized swelling, discoloration.

Portuguese Man-of-War

- Severe pain lasting hours, welts/rashes, possible breathing difficulties.

Treatment of Marine Animal Stings

General Principles

- Move victim from the water; calm them to prevent panic.
- Identify the type of sting quickly.

Jellyfish Stings

- Rinse with vinegar (not fresh water).
- Remove tentacles using tweezers/card edge.
- Heat immersion or hot water compress to reduce pain.

Stingray Stings

- Control bleeding; immerse wound in hot water (30–90 mins).

- Clean thoroughly, remove barb fragments if superficial, apply antibiotic ointment.

Sea Urchin Stings

- Remove visible spines carefully with tweezers.
- Soak area in hot water to ease pain.
- Cover wound, monitor for infection.

Portuguese Man-of-War

- Similar to jellyfish (vinegar or salt water rinse).
- Apply heat packs, watch for severe systemic symptoms.

Advanced Care

- Epinephrine for anaphylaxis, IV meds for severe cases.
- Tetanus shot updates, antibiotics if infection risk.

Key Takeaways

- **Prevention:** Protective gear, avoiding hazardous areas, knowledge of marine life.
- **Diagnosis:** Identify species (jellyfish, stingray, etc.), observe symptoms (pain, swelling, systemic issues).
- **Treatment:** Vinegar rinse for jellyfish, hot water immersion for stingrays, remove spines carefully, seek professional help if severe.

Chapter 39

FISHHOOKS INJURIES

Definition

- Puncture or laceration caused by a fishing hook, potentially embedding deep into skin, muscle, or tendon.

Prevention of Fishhook Injuries

Safe Handling of Gear

- Cover hooks with protective caps; store in tackle boxes.
- Use pliers or hemostats to handle hooks, ensure secure attachment to lines.

Casting Safety

- Check surroundings; avoid crowded areas or overhead obstacles.
- Signal others before casting.

Personal Protective Measures

- Wear long sleeves, gloves, protective eyewear.

- Closed-toe shoes to protect feet.

Education and Training

- Learn proper casting techniques.
- Familiarize with fishhook removal methods and basic wound care.

Diagnosis of Fishhook Injuries

Types of Injuries

- **Superficial:** Hook only in top layer of skin.
- **Embedded:** Deeper penetration into muscle/subcutaneous tissue.
- **Complex:** Hook near nerves, tendons, or critical structures (face, eyes, hands).

Signs and Symptoms

- Pain, redness, swelling at wound site.
- Possible numbness if nerves involved.
- Discharge or bleeding indicating infection or deeper injury.

Assessing Complications

- Infection risk (marine bacteria on hooks).
- Structural damage to tendons/nerves/blood vessels.
- Possible broken hook fragments.

Treatment of Fishhook Injuries

Fishing Injuries

A. Immediate First Aid
- **Assess the Wound**
  - Determine hook depth/location.
  - Check for severe pain, nerve/tendon damage.
- **Control Bleeding**
  - Apply gentle pressure with clean cloth/gauze.
- **Stabilize the Hook**
  - Minimize movement to avoid further tissue damage.
- **Clean the Area**
  - Rinse with clean water or saline to remove debris.

Removal Techniques

Superficial Hooks

- Gently back the hook out along entry path with pliers.
- Use String-Yank Technique if barb prevents smooth removal.

Embedded Hooks

1. String-Yank Technique
- Secure injured area, wrap strong string around hook curve.
- Press down on shank to disengage barb, yank string sharply.

- Avoid use near face/eyes or major structures.

2. Push-Through Technique

- Advance hook forward until barb emerges.
- Clip off barb, then withdraw hook backward.

3. Needle Cover Technique

- Insert a large-gauge needle along hook to cover barb.
- Withdraw hook and needle together.

4. Surgical Removal

- For hooks near critical structures (tendons, nerves, vessels).
- Seek professional medical help.

Wound Care After Removal

Clean the Wound

- Wash thoroughly with soap and water; apply antiseptic.

Dress the Wound

- Use sterile, non-stick bandage.
- Change dressing daily or if wet/soiled.

Pain Management

- OTC pain relievers (ibuprofen, acetaminophen).

Antibiotics & Infection Prevention

Topical Antibiotics

- Apply ointments (e.g., Neosporin).

Oral Antibiotics

- Consider for high-risk/marine wounds or infection signs.

Tetanus Vaccination

- Ensure up-to-date tetanus shot (booster if >5 years, or >10 years in low-risk).

When to Seek Medical Attention

Severe/Complex Injuries

- Retained hook fragments, tendon/nerve involvement.

Infection Signs

- Persistent redness, swelling, pus, fever/chills.

Critical Areas

- Involvement of eyes, face, hands.

Recovery & Monitoring

Signs of Healing

- Reduced pain, swelling, redness within days.

Follow-Up Care

- Reapply fresh dressings daily; avoid re-injury.

Long-Term Concerns

- Scar management, nerve damage, or chronic pain if improperly treated.

Key Takeaways

- **Prevention:** Safe gear handling, protective equipment, proper casting.
- **Diagnosis:** Evaluate hook depth/location, check for nerve/tendon damage.
- **Treatment:** Choose correct removal technique, focus on wound cleaning & infection control.
- **Medical Help:** For severe injuries, retained fragments, or infection.

Chapter 40

ALLERGIC REACTIONS

Definition & Common Triggers

- Immune overreaction to allergens (food, meds, insect stings, marine stings, environmental).
- Ranges from mild (itchy rash) to life-threatening (anaphylaxis).

Prevention of Allergic Reactions

Avoidance of Known Allergens

- Read food labels; avoid cross-contamination.
- Inform providers about drug allergies; wear alert bracelet.
- Protective gear for marine stings, reduce exposure to pollen/dust.

Strengthening Body Defenses

- Immunotherapy (allergy shots) for certain triggers.
- Antihistamines/nasal sprays during allergy season.

Emergency Preparedness

- Always carry an EpiPen if you have history of severe reactions.
- Keep antihistamines/steroids in first aid kits.

Diagnosis of Allergic Reactions

Clinical Evaluation

- Identify trigger, onset, previous episodes.
- Assess symptom severity (mild rash vs. systemic anaphylaxis).

Diagnostic Tests

- Skin prick tests, blood tests (IgE levels).
- Oral food challenges under supervision.
- Patch testing for contact dermatitis.

Treatment of Allergic Reactions

General Approaches

- **Mild:** Oral antihistamines, cool compresses.
- **Moderate:** Oral corticosteroids, topical steroids.
- **Severe (Anaphylaxis):** Immediate epinephrine injection, call emergency services.

Specific Treatments

- **Food Allergies:** Epinephrine for anaphylaxis, strict dietary avoidance.
- **Medication Allergies:** Discontinue offending drug, consider desensitization if essential.
- **Marine Stings:** Vinegar rinse (jellyfish), remove spines carefully, watch for systemic symptoms.

- **Contact Dermatitis:** Wash skin, topical steroids, antihistamines.
- **Environmental Allergies:** Antihistamines, nasal sprays, allergy shots.

Complications of Untreated Allergies

Anaphylaxis

- Airway swelling, low blood pressure, shock, potential fatality.

Infections

- Skin lesions can lead to bacterial infection.

Chronic Issues

- Persistent allergy symptoms (e.g., sinusitis, asthma exacerbations).

Key Takeaways

- **Prevention:** Avoid allergens, use protective measures, carry epinephrine if needed.
- **Diagnosis:** Clinical history, tests (skin prick, IgE).
- **Treatment:** Mild = antihistamines/steroids, Severe = epinephrine + emergency care.
- **Follow-Up:** Implement action plans, address triggers long-term.

Chapter 41

CARDIAC ARREST

Definition

- Blood flow to heart muscle blocked, causing tissue damage.
- Critical emergency requiring fast action, especially in remote ocean settings.

Prevention

Pre-Departure Screenings

- Medical evaluations for high-risk individuals (hypertension, diabetes, prior MI).
- Bring prescribed meds, keep them accessible.

Lifestyle & Activity Management

- Heart-healthy diet (low salt/saturated fats).
- Moderate exercise, limit alcohol/smoking.

Emergency Preparedness

- Essential supplies: Aspirin, nitroglycerin, AED, oxygen, blood pressure monitor.

- Crew trained in CPR/AED use.

Diagnosis of Heart Attack

Recognizing Symptoms

- Chest pressure/pain, possibly radiating to arms/jaw/back.
- Shortness of breath, cold sweats, nausea, lightheadedness.
- Atypical signs (fatigue, dizziness, indigestion-like discomfort).

Vital Sign Assessment

- Check heart rate, blood pressure, oxygen saturation.
- Pale, clammy skin indicates possible shock.

Treatment at Sea

Immediate Response

- Have patient rest; call captain/medical officer.
- Initiate mayday call or satellite communication for emergency guidance.

Medications

- **Aspirin:** 160–325 mg to chew (if no contraindications).
- **Nitroglycerin:** For chest pain if prescribed (max 3 doses, 5 mins apart).
- **Oxygen:** If SpO$_2$ <94%, give via mask or cannula.

Monitoring & Support

- Continuous check of vital signs; reassure patient.

- Keep warm, calm, reduce anxiety.

Advanced Care

- **AED:** If patient collapses or no pulse.
- **CPR:** 30 compressions : 2 breaths if unresponsive, no pulse.
- Prepare for potential evacuation to nearest port.

Post-Attack Monitoring

Observe for Recurrence

- Return of chest pain or instability.

Fluid Intake

- Small sips of water unless contraindicated.

Recovery Guidance

- Limit physical exertion.
- Continue necessary meds (e.g., beta-blockers) if available.

Key Takeaways

- **Prevention:** Screen high-risk individuals, maintain heart-healthy habits.
- **Diagnosis:** Recognize chest pain, shortness of breath, do vital sign checks.
- **Treatment:** Aspirin, nitroglycerin, oxygen, call for help, use AED if needed.
- **Evacuation:** Head toward medical facilities if symptoms worsen.

CHAPTER 42

RESPIRATORY DISTRESS

Definition

- Severe breathing difficulty due to asthma, smoke inhalation, or anaphylaxis.

Diagnosis

Common Signs

- Rapid breathing, wheezing/stridor, cyanosis, accessory muscle use.
- Oxygen saturation <94%.

Asthma Exacerbation

- Known history of asthma.
- Wheezing on exhalation, chest tightness, reduced PEFR.

Smoke Inhalation

- Exposure to fire/heavy smoke, soot in airway.

- Possible CO poisoning (confusion, headache, red skin).

Severe Allergic Reaction

- Recent allergen exposure, swelling of airway, hives.
- Rapid onset breathing difficulty, possible anaphylaxis.

Treatment

General Principles

- Sit patient upright, calm them.
- Provide oxygen if <94% SpO_2.
- Monitor vitals continuously.

Asthma

- **Short-Acting Beta-Agonists (SABAs):** Albuterol inhaler/nebulizer every 20 mins up to 3 doses first hour.
- **Corticosteroids:** Prednisone or similar.
- **Ipratropium Bromide** if severe.

Smoke Inhalation

- Airway management if swelling.
- 100% oxygen (non-rebreather) to displace CO.
- Bronchodilators if wheezing; possible IV fluids, manage burns/injuries.

Anaphylaxis

- **Epinephrine IM (0.3–0.5 mg)** into mid-thigh immediately.
- **Antihistamines (e.g., diphenhydramine), corticosteroids** if needed.
- Observe for biphasic reaction, prepare for airway management.

Supportive Care & Evacuation

Hydration

- IV fluids if low blood pressure or severe distress.

Pain Relief

- Acetaminophen or ibuprofen, avoiding respiratory depressants.

Psychological Support

- Reassure patient, reduce anxiety to improve breathing.

Evacuation

- Communicate with medical advisors; redirect vessel if needed.
- Priority if no response to initial treatments or severe airway compromise.

Long-Term Monitoring and Follow-Up
*(Applies especially to **Respiratory Distress** from Asthma, Smoke Inhalation, or Allergic Reactions)*

Observation After Treatment

- Monitor for recurrence of symptoms (e.g., biphasic anaphylaxis in allergic reactions).
- Continue oxygen therapy if indicated (e.g., after smoke inhalation or severe asthma attack).

Preventive Measures

- Ensure patients with asthma have rescue inhalers readily available.
- Educate all onboard about allergen avoidance and fire safety protocols.

- Restock any used medications and supplies immediately.

Key Takeaways
(For Asthma, Smoke Inhalation, and Allergic Reactions)

Asthma

- • Use albuterol (short-acting beta-agonist) for acute attacks.
- • Add corticosteroids (e.g., prednisone) if severity escalates.

Smoke Inhalation

- • Prioritize oxygen therapy to counteract potential carbon monoxide or airway damage.
- • Monitor for airway burns, edema, or respiratory failure.

Allergic Reactions

- Administer epinephrine **immediately** for anaphylaxis.
- Use antihistamines/steroids for additional support.

By following these measures, you can effectively manage **breathing difficulties** while awaiting advanced medical care in remote or maritime settings.

CHAPTER 43

SHOCK

Definition

- Critical condition where circulatory failure leads to inadequate tissue perfusion.

Causes and Types of Shock

Common Maritime Triggers

- Severe injury/trauma (falls, penetrating wounds).
- Blood loss (hypovolemic), dehydration.
- Cardiac issues (cardiogenic), e.g., heart attack.
- Anaphylaxis (allergic reactions).
- Sepsis from infected wounds (septic shock).
- Extreme emotional distress (neurogenic shock).

Prevention of Shock

Pre-Trip Preparations

- Health screenings for crew/passengers (cardiac, allergy history).

- Stock first aid kit: epinephrine auto-injectors, IV fluids, hemostatic agents.
- Crew training in CPR/AED use, hemorrhage control.

Safety Measures Onboard

- Secure equipment to prevent accidents in rough seas.
- Maintain hydration, manage allergens, ensure hygiene to prevent infections.

Diagnosis of Shock

Early Recognition

- Pale, clammy skin; weak/rapid pulse; rapid/shallow breathing; confusion.
- Low blood pressure, low or no urine output, extreme thirst.

Type-Specific Indicators

- **Hypovolemic:** Bleeding, dehydration signs, very rapid HR.
- **Cardiogenic:** Chest pain, arrhythmias, distended neck veins.
- **Anaphylactic:** Swelling, hives, difficulty breathing.
- **Septic:** Fever or hypothermia, possible infection source.
- **Neurogenic:** Low HR, warm/flushed skin below injury.

Treatment of Shock

General Emergency Response

- Lay patient flat, elevate legs ~12 inches (unless respiratory or head/spine injury).
- Provide oxygen (100% if possible).

- Control bleeding (direct pressure, tourniquet if limb-threatening).
- Administer IV fluids (saline, lactated Ringer's) unless cardiogenic shock is suspected.

Specific Treatments

- **Hypovolemic:** Aggressive fluid replacement, bleeding control.
- **Cardiogenic:** Nitroglycerin, aspirin for MI (if BP allows), minimal fluids.
- **Anaphylactic:** Epinephrine IM, antihistamines, corticosteroids.
- **Septic:** IV antibiotics (if available), fluid resuscitation.
- **Neurogenic:** Stabilize spine if trauma suspected, IV fluids, reassurance.

Emergency Evacuation

Contact Maritime Medical Support

- Use satellite phone or emergency radio for medical guidance.

Document Interventions

- Record vital signs, fluids given, medications administered.

Monitoring and Follow-Up

Continuous Vital Checks

- Pulse, BP, respiratory rate, oxygen saturation every 5–10 minutes.

Prepare for Port or Helicopter Evacuation

- Prioritize severe cases for nearest advanced care facility.

Key Takeaways

- **Prevention:** Safety measures, thorough first aid training, hydration, and allergy controls.
- **Diagnosis:** Recognize early signs (pale skin, rapid pulse, confusion).
- **Treatment:** Positioning, oxygen, IV fluids, control bleeding, treat the underlying cause.
- **Evacuation:** Contact professionals and be ready to move to advanced care.

CHAPTER 44

HEAD INJURIES

Definition & Causes

- Blunt trauma from falls, striking the head on surfaces, falling objects.
- Risk ranges from mild concussion to severe traumatic brain injury.

Diagnosis of Head Injuries

Assess Severity

- **Mild (Concussion):** Headache, dizziness, brief confusion, possible memory gaps.
- **Moderate/Severe:** Persistent vomiting, severe headache, loss of consciousness, unequal pupils, neurological deficits.

Glasgow Coma Scale (GCS)

- Eye opening (4–1), Verbal response (5–1), Motor response (6–1).
- Scores ≤8 = critical condition requiring urgent care.

Immediate Treatment

Stop Activity & Secure Environment

- Prevent further injury from boat movement or falls.

Positioning

- Lay flat, slight head elevation (20–30°) to reduce intracranial pressure.
- Avoid elevating legs unless in shock.

Control External Bleeding

- Gentle pressure with clean dressing (avoid heavy pressure if skull fracture suspected).

Monitor Vital Signs

- Pulse, respiration, BP every 5–10 minutes; use pulse oximeter if available.

Mild Injuries (Concussion)

Rest & Observation

- Quiet environment, limit physical/mental strain.

Pain Relief

- Acetaminophen for headaches (avoid NSAIDs to reduce bleeding risk).

Symptom Monitoring

- Watch for worsening confusion, persistent vomiting, or changes in vision.

Moderate to Severe Head Injuries

Neck/Spine Stabilization

- Assume possible cervical injury; use improvised collar or towels.

Oxygen Therapy

- If respiratory distress or low oxygen saturation.

IV Fluids

- Normal saline or lactated Ringer's; avoid large volumes (risk of cerebral edema).

Seizure Control

- Protect from injury if seizure occurs; use diazepam (if trained/available).

Long-Term Monitoring and Care

Neurological Checks

- Repeat GCS every 30 mins, watch for pupil changes.

Limit Activity

- No heavy lifting or straining; rest is crucial.

Prepare for Evacuation

- Contact medical professionals if signs worsen; head to nearest port with advanced care.

Emergency Preparedness

Kit Essentials

- Sterile gauze, pulse oximeter, BP monitor, cervical collar or materials to improvise.
- Pain relievers (acetaminophen), anticonvulsants (if trained).

Crew Training

- Basic first aid, head injury assessment, emergency response protocols.

Key Takeaways

- **Immediate Response:** Control bleeding, stabilize neck, monitor vitals.
- **Mild Injuries:** Rest and observe carefully for 24–48 hours.
- **Severe Injuries:** Neck immobilization, oxygen, possible IV fluids, urgent evacuation.
- **Evacuation Protocols:** Seek advanced care for altered consciousness, neurological deficits, or worsening symptoms.

CHAPTER 45

INFECTIONS

Cause: Cuts, scrapes, or wounds exposed to saltwater, dirt, or poor hygiene.

Risk: Swelling, redness, fever; can progress to serious complications (cellulitis, sepsis).

Understanding Wound Infections

Causes

- Marine bacteria (Vibrio, Pseudomonas) from saltwater.
- Contamination by dirt, grease, or poor hygiene.
- Delayed or improper wound care.

Types

- **Superficial:** Localized redness/pain.
- **Deep Tissue:** Cellulitis, abscess.
- **Systemic:** Sepsis, necrotizing fasciitis.

Diagnosis of Wound Infections

Clinical Assessment

- Early signs: Redness, warmth, swelling, pain, discharge.
- Worsening signs: Spread of redness (cellulitis), fluctuance (abscess).
- Systemic: Fever, chills, tachycardia, hypotension (shock).

High-Risk Indicators

- Saltwater exposure (Vibrio, Aeromonas).
- Chronic conditions (diabetes) or poor circulation.

Immediate Treatment

General Principles

- Clean wounds thoroughly ASAP.
- Use sterile gloves and equipment.

Wound Care Procedure

- Flush with saline/clean water, mild soap around edges.
- Debride dead tissue if trained.
- Apply antiseptics (povidone-iodine, chlorhexidine).
- Dress with sterile, non-stick gauze; change daily.

Antibiotics and Treatment

When to Use Antibiotics

- Mild, superficial: Topical antibiotics might suffice.
- Moderate (cellulitis): Oral antibiotics.
- Severe (sepsis/necrotizing): IV antibiotics.

Selecting Antibiotics

- **Common Skin Bacteria:** Cephalexin or Dicloxacillin.
- **Marine-Related (Vibrio):** Doxycycline or ceftriaxone, levofloxacin.
- **MRSA:** Trimethoprim-sulfamethoxazole or clindamycin.

Administration & Duration

- Oral for moderate infections (3–7 days).
- IV for severe, rapidly spreading or septic cases (10–14 days).

Advanced Care

Abscess Management

- Incision & Drainage (I&D); sterile technique.

Necrotizing Fasciitis

- High-dose IV antibiotics, emergency debridement.

Sepsis

- Broad-spectrum IV antibiotics, IV fluids, urgent evacuation.

Monitoring & Long-Term Care

Signs of Improvement

- Reduced redness, swelling, pain, normalizing temperature.

Prevention of Recurrence

- Proper hygiene, avoiding saltwater exposure on open wounds.

Evacuation Criteria

Severe or Unresponsive Infections

- Rapid progression, systemic signs of shock.
- Consult maritime medical services.

Key Takeaways

- **Early Intervention**: Clean, disinfect promptly.
- **Appropriate Antibiotics**: Chosen by likely pathogens/severity.
- **Emergency Preparedness**: Stock necessary meds, supplies.
- **Evacuation**: For severe, uncontrolled infections.

Chapter 46

DIABETIC EMERGENCIES

Types of Emergencies

Hypoglycemia (Low Blood Sugar)

- Causes: Insufficient food, excessive insulin, strenuous activity.
- Symptoms: Sweating, shaking, confusion; <70 mg/dL.

Hyperglycemia (High Blood Sugar)

- Causes: Missed insulin, excess carbs, infection.
- Symptoms: Thirst, frequent urination, fatigue; >180 mg/dL.

Diabetic Ketoacidosis (DKA)

- Causes: Prolonged hyperglycemia => ketone buildup.
- Symptoms: Fruity breath, deep breathing, vomiting; often >250 mg/dL.

Diagnosis

Blood Sugar Testing

- Glucometer, test strips.

- Normal: 70–100 mg/dL fasting, <120 mg/dL post-meal.

Physical Exam

- Hypo: Pale, clammy skin, tachycardia.
- Hyper: Dry mouth, possibly fruity breath (DKA).

Treatment

Hypoglycemia

- **Mild/Moderate**: 15–20 g fast-acting carbs (glucose tabs, juice). Recheck in 15 mins, repeat if <70 mg/dL.
- **Severe**: Glucagon IM (1 mg) if unconscious; turn on side, call for help.

Hyperglycemia

- Increase fluids (water), administer insulin if prescribed.
- Recheck glucose in 1–2 hours.

DKA

- IV fluids (normal saline), insulin if trained.
- Watch for dehydration, electrolyte imbalance, urgent evacuation if severe.

Emergency Preparedness

Onboard Supplies

- Glucometer + extra strips, glucagon kit, insulin + syringes/pens, quick carbs.

Crew Training

- Recognize early signs, administer glucose or glucagon, follow sliding-scale insulin instructions.

Prevention

Regular Monitoring
- Check BG levels before meals/bed, after exercise.

Meal Planning
- Balanced carbs, proteins, consistent schedule.

Evacuation

Severe, Unresponsive Cases
- Unconscious or suspected DKA => immediate medical evacuation.

Key Takeaways

- **Hypo:** Fast carbs, glucagon if unconscious.
- **Hyper:** Hydration, insulin; watch for DKA.
- **Be Prepared:** Stock glucose, insulin, train crew.
- **Evacuate:** If severe or unresponsive.

Chapter 47

FIRST AID ESSENTIALS

General Wound Care & Dressings

Sterile Gauze Pads (various sizes)

- Cover wounds, prevent infection.

Adhesive Bandages (waterproof)

- Small cuts/abrasions.

Elastic Bandages

- Support sprains, secure dressings.

Non-Adherent Dressings

- For burns or wounds that shouldn't stick.

Adhesive Medical Tape

- Secures gauze/dressings.

Antiseptics & Cleaning

Saline Solution

- Flushing debris or salt from wounds.

Antiseptic Solutions

- Povidone-iodine, chlorhexidine to disinfect.

Hydrogen Peroxide (3%)

- Limited use on deep wounds.

Antibiotic Ointments

- Prevent infection in minor wounds.

Medications

Pain/Fever

- Paracetamol (acetaminophen), ibuprofen.

Allergy/Anaphylaxis

- Antihistamines (diphenhydramine), EpiPen for severe reactions.

GI Meds

- Antacids, anti-diarrheals, ORS, anti-nausea meds.

Antibiotics

- Broad-spectrum oral (amoxicillin-clavulanate, doxycycline).
- Topical for minor wounds.

Tools & Equipment

Monitoring Devices
- Digital thermometer, BP monitor, pulse oximeter.

Emergency Tools
- Scissors, tweezers, hemostatic forceps, irrigation syringe.

Splints & Immobilization
- SAM splint, triangular bandages, cervical collar.

Specialized Marine Supplies

Vinegar
- Neutralize jellyfish stings.

Hot Packs
- Pain relief for stingray, sea urchin stings.

Burn Dressings
- For scalds, contact with hot surfaces/fluids.

Emergency Response Equipment

CPR Mask or Shield
- Safe rescue breathing.

AED (Automated External Defibrillator)
- Cardiac emergencies (sudden arrest).

Airway Management

- Bag-valve mask, oropharyngeal airways.

Oxygen Supply

- Portable cylinder, masks, cannulas.

Documentation & Communication

Medical Guidebook

- Step-by-step instructions for common emergencies.

First Aid Logbook

- Record treatments, meds given, vitals.

Emergency Contacts

- Maritime medical assistance, local ER.

Key Considerations

Maintenance

- Check expiry dates, restock used items.

Crew Training

- Basic first aid, CPR, AED use.

Customization

- Tailor kit to crew size, trip length, marine hazards.

CHAPTER 48

TRANSPORTING AN INJURED PERSON

Planning the Evacuation

Assess Severity

- Potential need for immediate medical intervention.

Resources & Modes of Transport

- Helicopter/airlift for severe trauma.
- Boat transfer to shore ambulance if stable.

Preparing the Patient

Stabilize Before Moving

- Control bleeding, immobilize fractures, secure airway.

Spinal Precautions

- Use cervical collar/backboard if neck/spine injury suspected.

Monitor Vital Signs

- Regular checks (BP, pulse, respiration, SpO_2) during transfer.

Communication & Coordination

Contact Medical Facilities

- Alert receiving hospital about patient's condition, ETA.
- Provide vital info (age, injury type, treatments given).

Satellite/Radio Comms

- Maintain contact with maritime medical advisors.
- Update position and patient status.

Types of Transport

Ship-to-Ship Transfer

- If a rescue vessel is better equipped/closer.
- Coordinate stable sea conditions for safe transfer.

Ship-to-Shore via Small Boat

- Ensure stable conditions, patient secured on a stretcher.

Air Evacuation (Helicopter)

- Life-threatening injuries requiring rapid response.
- Clear a safe landing/pickup area if possible.

During Transport

Maintain Stability

- Secure the stretcher, ensure minimal jostling.
- Continue IV fluids, oxygen if needed.

Reassess Regularly

- Watch for shock, changes in consciousness, airway compromise.

Post-Transfer Handover

Medical Handover

- Provide full report: injury details, treatments, vitals, timeline.
- Give logbook/notes to receiving medical team.

Crew Debrief

- Review efficiency, safety, and needed improvements for future.

Key Takeaways

- **Stabilize First:** Ensure bleeding control, airway, immobilization before transit.
- **Plan & Communicate:** Notify nearest medical center, maintain contact en route.
- **Safe Transport:** Choose best mode (boat, helicopter) based on injury severity and conditions.
- **Documentation:** Keep detailed records, relay info accurately to receiving facility.

Assessing the Situation

Evaluate the Severity of the Injury

Mild Injuries (e.g., minor cuts, sprains, mild dehydration)

- Treat onboard; evacuation usually not needed unless complications arise.

Moderate to Severe Injuries (e.g., fractures, severe burns, head trauma, serious infections)

- May require timely evacuation for advanced medical care.

Critical Emergencies (e.g., heart attacks, severe bleeding, anaphylaxis)

- Immediate evacuation is necessary; advanced support en route often required.

Identify Immediate Needs

Stabilization: Control bleeding, maintain airway, provide pain relief.

Monitoring: Assign someone to track vital signs during transit.

Preparing for Evacuation

Communication

- **Contact Emergency Services** (e.g., Coast Guard, port authority, maritime medical advisors) via satellite phone, VHF radio, etc.
- **Provide Detailed Information**: Patient's condition, location, onboard resources.

Patient Stabilization

- **Immobilization**: Splints, cervical collars, backboards for spinal injuries.
- **Pain Management**: Appropriate medications while avoiding those that compromise respiration.
- **Airway and Breathing**: Oxygen supply, airway adjuncts for respiratory distress.
- **Hemorrhage Control**: Direct pressure or tourniquets for severe bleeding.

Types of Transportation

Ship-to-Shore Evacuation

Coast Guard Assistance:
- Helicopter rescue for critical patients.
- Rescue boats for moderate cases closer to shore.

Transfer to a Smaller Vessel:
- If the main ship can't reach port, move the patient to a faster, smaller vessel.
- Secure stretchers; avoid unnecessary movement.

Helicopter Evacuation
- **Criteria**: For critical injuries or remote locations.
- **Arrangements**: Clear landing zone or use a hoist if landing isn't possible.
- **Patient Preparation**: Secure in stretcher/basket, protect from hypothermia.

Ambulance or Ground Transport
- **Onshore Coordination**: Ambulance ready at the evacuation point; share patient's condition and onboard treatment details.

Key Equipment for Transport

Stretcher Types
- **Rigid Stretchers**: Full immobilization (e.g., suspected spinal injuries).
- **Basket Stretchers**: Suitable for helicopter rescues/hoisting.

- **Soft Stretchers**: Lightweight, easier handling in tight spaces.

Monitoring and Support

- **Vital Signs Monitors**: Heart rate, blood pressure, oxygen saturation.
- **Oxygen Supply**: Portable cylinders, masks, or nasal cannulas.
- **First Aid Kit**: Bandages, splints, medications, airway tools.

Transporting the Patient Safely

Securing the Patient

- Strap patient to stretcher; use padding to minimize movement.
- Protect from environmental elements (e.g., hypothermia, seawater).

Monitoring During Transit

- **Assign a Caregiver**: Monitor vitals, provide interventions.
- **Reassess Regularly**: Breathing, pulse, consciousness.

Documentation and Handover

Medical Report

- Include patient's history, allergies, injury/illness details, treatments given, and vital signs trends.
- Share with receiving team to maintain continuity of care.

Patient Handover
- Give a clear verbal summary upon transfer.
- Provide written medical records and any test results.

Challenges and Mitigation

Rough Seas
- **Challenge**: Instability during handling.
- **Solution**: Secure patient, stabilize stretcher, use anti-slip mats.

Remote Locations
- **Challenge**: Delayed response from emergency services.
- **Solution**: Maintain communication with maritime medical advisors, stabilize and support patient until help arrives.

Communication Barriers
- **Challenge**: Poor communication infrastructure.
- **Solution**: Use satellite phones, VHF radios, emergency beacons for reliable contact.

Emergency Preparedness for Future Incidents

- **First Aid Training**: Crew members trained in advanced first aid and CPR.
- **Evacuation Drills**: Practice patient transfer procedures regularly.
- **Equipment Maintenance**: Regular checks of stretchers, oxygen tanks, and medical kits.
- **Pre-Established Protocols**: Clear plans for evacuation based on the ship's setup and available resources.

Key Takeaways

- **Preparation**: Stock appropriate medical supplies; maintain emergency communication tools.
- **Assessment**: Accurately gauge injury severity to determine urgency.
- **Transport Options**: Choose helicopters, rescue boats, or ambulances based on injury level and location.
- **Safety**: Prioritize stabilizing and securing the patient throughout transfer.
- **Communication**: Thorough reporting ensures seamless care from ship to shore.

PART EIGHT

NAVIGATIONAL ERRORS

CHAPTER 49

CORRECTING COURSE MISTAKES

1. Causes of Navigational Mistakes

Human Error

- Fatigue (long shifts, insufficient rest)
- Inexperience (lack of training, unfamiliarity with vessel/ equipment)
- Poor Decision-Making (not following proper protocols)
- Distraction (inattention to instruments or external conditions)

Equipment Failure

- Malfunctioning Instruments (GPS, radar, compass)
- Loss of Communication (radio or satellite systems)
- Power Outages (impacting electronic navigation systems)

Environmental Conditions

- Adverse Weather (storms, fog, high winds)
- Uncharted Hazards (reefs, rocks, sandbars)
- Strong Currents or Tides (unexpected course deviations)

2. Potential Consequences

Grounding

- Occurs when the vessel hits the seabed or underwater obstacles.
- Risks include hull damage, flooding, and environmental harm (fuel spills).

Collisions

- Possible with other vessels, offshore structures, or obstacles.
- Can cause severe structural damage, fires, explosions, or loss of life.

Allision

- Collision with stationary objects (piers, buoys).
- Leads to damage to the vessel and navigational aids.

Deviation from Planned Course

- Results in delays or entry into restricted waters.
- Potential for legal/financial penalties and higher operational costs.

3. Corrective Actions for Navigational Emergencies

Immediate Actions

- Assess the situation (use radar, GPS, visual checks).
- Alert the crew (assign roles, responsibilities).
- Reduce speed (minimize damage or risk).

Correcting the Course

- Verify position (use backup GPS, paper charts).
- Adjust course (plot a new route, use manual steering if autopilot fails).
- Consult navigation aids (lighthouses, buoys, coastal radar).

Managing Equipment Failures

- Switch to backup systems (spare GPS, manual compass).
- Attempt repairs (if crew skills/tools allow).
- Communicate with nearby vessels (seek assistance or hazard info).

Responding to Grounding

- Check for damage (hull breaches, flooding).
- Refloat vessel if possible (reverse slowly, use anchors).
- Request assistance (Coast Guard, local authorities).

Preventing Collisions

- Use emergency steering (manually steer away from threats).
- Issue collision warnings (horn, light signals).
- Communicate with other ships (coordinate via VHF radio).

4. Long-Term Preventive Measures

Training and Education

- Regular crew training in navigation and emergency response.
- Conduct simulations to practice emergency scenarios.

Equipment Maintenance

- Frequent inspections (navigation systems, compasses, communication tools).

- Keep spare equipment/paper charts onboard.

Navigational Protocols

- Pre-departure planning (detailed route, shared with crew).
- Redundancy (cross-check electronic data with visual references).
- Constant monitoring (dedicated personnel on watch).

Communication

- Establish contact points (coastal stations, rescue services).
- Practice emergency signals (MAYDAY, PAN-PAN).

5. Emergency Evacuation Considerations

- Prepare lifesaving equipment (lifeboats, rafts, PFDs).
- Follow abandon-ship protocol if necessary.
- Notify authorities (location, number of people onboard).

6. Key Takeaways

- Causes include human error, equipment failure, and environmental factors.
- Consequences range from grounding and collisions to legal/financial penalties.
- Corrective actions focus on assessing, stabilizing, and using backup systems.
- Prevention requires ongoing training, maintenance, and strong navigational protocols.
- Emergency response might involve outside assistance and potential evacuation.

DEALING WITH EQUIPMENT FAILURE

1. Types of Navigational Equipment & Potential Failures

- GPS (signal loss, incorrect readings)
- Radar (malfunction or inability to detect obstacles)
- Compass (magnetic or gyroscopic failure)
- ECDIS (software glitches, power loss)
- VHF/Satellite Comms (loss of communication)
- Autopilot (inaccurate navigation or course maintenance)
- Depth Sounder (failure to detect underwater hazards)

2. Common Causes of Equipment Failure

- Environmental factors (weather extremes, corrosion)
- Human error (incorrect setup, lack of maintenance)
- Mechanical/electrical issues (power fluctuations, wear and tear)
- Software/system errors (glitches, outdated firmware)

3. Steps to Address Equipment Failures

- General troubleshooting (identify faulty system, check power, reset)
- Backup systems/alternatives (paper charts, handheld compass, visual lookouts)
- Immediate risk mitigation (reduce speed, alert crew, switch to manual operations)

4. Immediate Actions to Mitigate Risk

- Stabilize the situation (reduce speed, alert the crew)
- Use redundant system (activate backup devices, refer to printed nautical charts)
- Communicate with nearby vessels (secondary communication tools, alert other vessels of the issue)

5. Preventive Measures

- Equipment maintenance (regular checks, repair/replace corroded parts)
- Crew training (manual navigation, drills)
- Redundancy (backup GPS, radios, paper charts)
- Software updates (maintain current versions, ensure compatibility)

6. Long-Term Strategies

- Post-failure analysis (document root causes to prevent recurrence)
- Maintenance schedule (routine inspections, compliance logs)
- Equipment upgrades (modern systems with built-in redundancies)

CHAPTER 51

PREVENTING COLLISIONS

Common Causes of Collisions

- Human factors (lack of vigilance, fatigue, inexperience, poor communication)
- Navigational errors (ignoring COLREGs, misjudging distance/speed)
- Environmental conditions (fog, storms, strong currents)
- Equipment failures (faulty radar, lost communication)

Dos and Don'ts for Collision Prevention

Dos

- Maintain a proper lookout (dedicated watch, binoculars, radar).
- Follow COLREGs (understand give-way/stand-on rules).
- Use navigational aids (radar, AIS, GPS, visual checks).
- Communicate clearly (VHF radio, confirm intentions).
- Reduce speed in risky conditions (fog, heavy traffic).

- Practice effective watchkeeping (avoid fatigue, rotate crew).
- Plan and update routes (avoid congested areas, adjust for weather).

Don'ts

- Ignore COLREGs (never assume others will yield automatically).
- Rely solely on technology (cross-check visually and manually).
- Neglect communication (failing to clarify actions with nearby vessels).
- Overlook environmental conditions (fog, storms, restricted visibility).
- Allow fatigue (long, unbroken shifts reduce alertness).

Advanced Techniques & Technologies for Collision Avoidance

- AIS (real-time vessel data for better awareness).
- Radar systems (detect nearby objects, confirm visually).
- ECDIS (integrates multiple navigational data sources).
- Sound signals (blasts to indicate maneuvers, especially in fog).
- Emergency maneuvering (emergency stops/turns, alert crew).

Long-Term Strategies to Prevent Collisions

- Crew training (collision avoidance exercises, COLREGs education).
- Maintenance (routine checks, backups for navigation and communication).

- Route planning (avoid busy shipping lanes, monitor weather patterns).

Key Takeaways Across All Sections

- Navigational errors stem from human error, equipment failure, and environmental factors.
- Corrective/preventive measures include crew training, diligent watchkeeping, and equipment maintenance.
- Equipment failure management calls for rapid troubleshooting, backup systems, and clear communication.
- Collision prevention relies on following COLREGs, maintaining situational awareness, and communicating intentions.
- Emergency preparedness (evacuation plans, lifesaving equipment, coordinated response) is crucial if all else fail

PART NINE

COMMUNICATION AND RESCUE

CHAPTER 52

USING MARINE RADIOS EFFECTIVELY

Purpose of Marine Radio Communication

Safety

- Used for emergency calls (MAYDAY, PAN-PAN), weather updates.

Navigation

- Contact marinas, locks, and bridges; request navigational assistance.

Routine Communication

- Coordinate maneuvers and update other vessels or crew.

Commercial Use (Large Boats)

- Cargo coordination, scheduling, and compliance with maritime regulations.

Types of Marine Radios

VHF Marine Radios

- Most common on boats of all sizes; line-of-sight range;

designated channels (e.g., Channel 16 for distress).

HF/SSB Radios

- High-frequency, long-distance communication (thousands of miles).

Handheld Radios

- Portable units for small boats or backup use on larger vessels; shorter range.

Basic Radio Communication Procedures

General Rules

- Listen before transmitting; keep messages short and clear; use proper channels.

Making a Call

- Identify the vessel being called; wait for response; switch to a working channel for routine conversation.

Emergency Calls

- MAYDAY (life-threatening), PAN-PAN (urgent), SECURITÉ (safety information).

Differences Between Small and Large Boats

Small Boats

- Typically use VHF (fixed or handheld); focus on short-range safety and navigation.

Large Boats

- Often have multiple systems (VHF, HF/SSB, satellite); must meet regulatory requirements for commercial operations.

Best Practices for Effective Communication

- Familiarize yourself with common channels and standard phrases.
- Monitor Channel 16 (distress/hailing) when underway.
- Maintain professional etiquette, minimize unnecessary chatter.
- Test equipment regularly to ensure functionality.

Regulatory Requirements

Licensing

- Recreational boaters may not need a license domestically, but station licenses are required for certain commercial or international voyages.

Identification

- MMSI numbers for DSC-enabled radios on large vessels.

GMDSS Compliance

- Mandatory for vessels engaged in certain international voyages.

Chapter 53

AIS (AUTOMATIC IDENTIFICATION SYSTEM)

AIS Overview

Key Features of AIS

Vessel Tracking:
- Uses GPS to broadcast position, speed, heading.
- Allows port authorities & other ships to track movements.

Data Exchange:
- Operates on VHF frequencies; transmits/receives within ~20–30 NM range (terrestrial) or via satellite for global.

Data Types:
- **Static**: Ship name, IMO, MMSI, size, type.
- **Dynamic**: Position, speed, course, heading.
- **Voyage**: Destination, ETA, draught.

How AIS Works

Transponders:
- Class A (large ships; more frequent updates), Class B (smaller vessels).

Receiving Stations:
- Ships, shore stations, satellites display AIS data on charts/radar.

Collision Avoidance:
- Real-time awareness of nearby vessels reduces collision risk.

Applications of AIS

Safety:
- Improves situational awareness, aids search/rescue.

Port & Traffic Management:
- Optimizes berthing, scheduling, overall traffic flow.

Environmental Monitoring:
- Tracks vessels for emission zones, pollution control.

Global Shipping & Security:
- Monitors illegal fishing, smuggling, piracy.

Limitations of AIS

Signal Range:
- VHF-based range is limited; satellite AIS can extend coverage but may have congestion delays.

Reliance on User Input:

- Manually entered data (destination, ETA) can be outdated or incorrect.

Overcrowding:

- High-traffic zones can cause signal congestion.

Buying, Registering, and Installing AIS

Selecting an AIS Device

Types:

- **Class A**: Higher power, frequent updates (commercial).
- **Class B**: Lower power, less frequent updates (recreational).
- **Receive-Only**: Displays other vessels' AIS but does not transmit own data.

Key Considerations:

- Boat's power source (12V or 24V).
- Integration with chart plotter/MFD.
- GPS antenna (internal vs. external).
- VHF antenna splitter if sharing with radio.

Purchasing the AIS Device

Reputable Brands:

- Garmin, Simrad, Raymarine, Furuno, Vesper Marine.

Buying Channels:

- Marine electronics stores or online.

Professional Advice:

- Consider consulting a marine electronics expert for best fit.

Registering Your AIS

Obtain an MMSI Number:

- Unique ID for your vessel.
- In the U.S.: FCC (international) or organizations like TowBoatUS for domestic.
- Other countries: National maritime authority.

Registration:

- Submit vessel/owner info, emergency contacts, etc. to local authorities.

Installing the AIS System

Mounting & Connections:

- Install the transponder near nav equipment in a dry spot.
- Attach GPS antenna with clear sky view.
- Use a VHF antenna or splitter.
- Integrate with chart plotter/radar (NMEA 0183 or NMEA 2000).

Professional Installation:

- Recommended if unsure about wiring or system config.

Configuring the AIS

Programming:
- Enter MMSI, ship name, dimensions, etc.
- Optionally input voyage data (draft, destination).

Testing:
- Perform dockside tests for transmit/receive functionality.
- Check integration with other onboard devices.

Ongoing Maintenance & Compliance

Software Updates:
- Keep AIS firmware current.

Inspections:
- Check antenna, power cables, data connections.

Legal Requirements:
- Comply with local/international laws for AIS usage.

Costs
- AIS Unit: $300–$3,000
- GPS/Antenna Splitter: $50–$300
- MMSI Registration: Free/nominal fee
- Professional Install: $100–$500+

Marine Traffic App Integration

Real-Time Vessel Tracking

Live Position Updates:
- See AIS-equipped vessels on a map, manage fleets.

Collision Avoidance:
- Identify traffic in busy waterways.

Navigation & Route Planning

Weather Overlays:
- Access wind, waves, and forecasts to plan safer routes.

Port Information:
- Check traffic, arrivals/departures, anchorage status.

Historical Data & Playback

Route History:
- Review vessel movements for analysis, incident reviews.

Incident Analysis:
- Playback AIS records to understand collisions/ emergencies.

Geofencing & Alerts

Custom Alerts:
- Notifications for vessels entering/exiting zones.

Proximity Warnings:

- Real-time approach warnings.

Search & Rescue Assistance

Emergency Situations:

- Locate vessels in distress via AIS signals.

Missing Boats:

- Track AIS data for overdue/missing vessels.

Environmental & Regulatory Compliance

Avoid Restricted Zones:

- Identify no-entry areas or emission control zones.

Compliance Monitoring:

- Ensure vessel meets AIS mandates and environmental regs.

Community & Collaboration

Crowdsourced Data:

- Contribute AIS data to global database.

Networking:

- Marine industry professionals, enthusiasts share info/ resources.

Cost Efficiency

Fuel Optimization:

- Plan routes considering weather, traffic.

Maintenance Planning:

- Use historical tracking/performance data to schedule upkeep.

User-Friendly Features

Accessibility:

- Available on mobile, tablet, desktop.

Custom Map Overlays:

- Vessel types, routes, weather layers are selectable.

Key Takeaways

1. AIS Fundamentals:

- Transmits/receives vessel data (position, speed, course) on VHF channels or via satellite.
- Enhances collision avoidance, traffic management, and maritime security.

2. Purchasing & Registering AIS:

- Choose **Class A** (commercial) or **Class B** (recreational) as needed.
- Obtain MMSI number, mount equipment properly, integrate with onboard electronics, and follow local regulations.

3. Installing & Configuring:

- Proper **GPS antenna** placement and **VHF splitter** usage.
- Input correct vessel info, test transmissions, keep firmware updated.

4. Marine Traffic App:

- Complements AIS by providing **real-time vessel tracking**, historical playback, weather overlays, and alerts.
- Useful for collision avoidance, route planning, security, and environmental compliance.
- By leveraging a well-chosen AIS system and apps like Marine Traffic, boaters can significantly improve situational awareness, safety, and operational efficiency on the water.

Chapter 54

FLARES, FLAGS AND LIGHTS

Flares: Aerial and Handheld Signals

Types

- Aerial (parachute, meteor), handheld, smoke.

Role

- Attract attention (distress signal), visible day or night, red color for emergency.

Best Practices

- Follow manufacturer instructions, store properly, check expiration dates.

Regulatory Requirements

- Most boats must carry approved flares; SOLAS standards for international voyages.

Flags: Traditional and Effective Signaling

Types

- Distress Signal Flag (square flag with ball/circle below), Code Flags (e.g., N+C for distress).

Role

- Daytime signaling, universal recognition, can supplement other signals.

Best Practices

- Hoist flags high for visibility, keep them clean and undamaged.

Lights: Continuous and Intermittent Signals

Types

- Strobe lights, flashlights, navigation lights, searchlights.

Role

- Essential at night or in low visibility, flashing patterns recognized as distress signals.

Best Practices

- Conserve battery power, aim for maximum visibility, combine with radio or flags.

Regulatory Requirements

- Strobes and other emergency lights often required on life rafts and PFDs.

Choosing the Right Signaling Method

Flares – Long-range visibility, day/night use.

Flags – Daytime visibility, easy deployment.

Lights – Nighttime or low-visibility signaling, longer duration than flares.

Summary of Use Cases

Signaling Method	Best For	Time of Use	Visibility Range
Flares	Long-distance signaling	Day Night	Up to 10 miles (aerial) Up to 40 miles (aerial)
Flags	Traditional distress signaling	Daytime	Line-of-sight
Lights	Nighttime signaling, prolonged use	Nighttime or low visibility	Varies (up to several miles)

Conclusion

Flares, flags, and lights form a versatile trio for marine signaling, each suited to different conditions. Proper usage, maintenance, and adherence to regulations are vital for effective distress signaling.

Chapter 55

HAND SIGNALS AND AUDIBLE SIGNALS

Hand Signals

Purpose

- Non-verbal communication when verbal/radio methods fail; standardized for universal understanding.

Common Maritime Hand Signals

- Wave arms overhead for distress; pointing to direct attention; clenched fist to stop; raised open palm for attention; thumbs up/down to signal approval or rejection.

Use in Specific Scenarios

- Search and Rescue (SAR), crew coordination in noisy conditions.

Audible Signals

Purpose

- Effective in fog, heavy rain, or at night; can travel farther than hand/visual signals.

Types

- Whistles (short, repeated blasts for distress), fog horns (prolonged blasts for positioning or 5 short blasts for danger), bells/gongs, shouting.

Maritime Regulations

- COLREGs Rule 34: short and prolonged blasts to signal course changes or danger.

Combined Use of Hand & Audible Signals

- Essential for coordinating SAR; man overboard scenarios; deck emergencies.
- Hand signals guide rescuers visually; whistles/fog horns draw attention.

Best Practices for Using Hand and Audible Signals

- Learn standard signals, practice in drills, equip all life jackets with whistles, maintain functional horns/bells.

Advantages & Limitations

Method	Advantages	Limitations
Hand Signals	Visible in good light; simple	Ineffective in fog/dark; need line-of-sight
Audible Signals	Effective in poor visibility/fog	Limited by noise; directional source may be unclear

Conclusion

Hand and audible signals are vital backups in emergencies. They ensure communication when electronic means fail, enhancing overall maritime safety.

Chapter 56

PORTABLE EMERGENCY DEVICES

Purpose: This chapter provides a comprehensive guide to life-saving portable tools that should be included in any vessel's emergency kit. These devices support **communication**, **tracking**, **navigation**, and **survival** when conventional systems fail or during abandonment scenarios.

Communication and Signaling Devices

These tools are critical for initiating rescue operations by transmitting distress signals and communicating with other vessels or agencies.

EPIRB (Emergency Position-Indicating Radio Beacon)

- **Primary Function:** Transmits an emergency distress signal to satellites operated by the COSPAS-SARSAT system.

- **Activation:** Manual or automatic (usually activates upon water immersion).
- **Transmission:** Sends on 406 MHz to satellites and a 121.5 MHz homing signal for close-range detection by SAR teams.
- **Range:** Global.
- **Power:** Long-lasting lithium batteries (5–7 years shelf life, 24+ hours operational).
- **Best Use:** For whole-vessel emergencies; typically mounted but portable models exist.
- **Lifesaving Value:** One of the most essential tools for long-distance offshore voyages.

PLB (Personal Locator Beacon)

Definition: A compact, personal-sized version of an EPIRB, often worn or carried.

Key Features:

- Manually activated.
- GPS-enabled for precise location transmission.
- 5–7 year battery, 24+ hours of signal time.
- Global coverage; no subscription required.
- Often waterproof, some models float and include strobe lights.

Top Devices:

- **ACR ResQLink View 425:** Best overall—floating, display, strobe.
- **Ocean Signal rescueME PLB1:** Smallest unit—needs flotation pouch.
- **ACR ResQLink 400:** Budget-friendly, full GPS, strobe, floating.

- **McMurdo FastFind 220:** Most durable—6-year battery, rugged.
- **Garmin inReach Mini 2:** For two-way text + GPS tracking (subscription required).

When to Use: MOB (man overboard), vessel loss, disorientation at sea.

VHF Marine Radio (Handheld, Waterproof)

Purpose: Short-range real-time communication with other vessels, Coast Guard, or marinas.

Why It's Essential:
- Operates where there is no cell coverage.
- Coast Guard constantly monitors Channel 16.

Top Features:
- Waterproof (IPX7/IPX8).
- Floating.
- DSC-enabled for distress calls.
- Some include GPS for sending location.
- Dual/triple-watch mode.
- 5–6 watt power output, 8–12-mile range.

Best Units:
- **Standard Horizon HX890:** High-end GPS, DSC, float, weather, 11+ hours.
- **Icom IC-M94D:** Built-in GPS & DSC, long battery, reliable.
- **Cobra MR HH600:** Budget with Bluetooth, GPS.
- **Uniden MHS75:** Inexpensive, reliable, no GPS.

Best For: All vessel sizes, especially small crafts and tenders.

Satellite Phones (Iridium, Inmarsat, Garmin inReach)

Use Case: Works beyond VHF/cellular range. Enables global communication and SOS services.

Capabilities:

- Make emergency calls or send texts.
- GPS-enabled with SOS activation.
- Can receive weather updates and email.
- Rechargeable, often compatible with solar.

Best Models:

- **Iridium Extreme 9575:** Toughest, SOS button, GPS, 100% global.
- **Inmarsat IsatPhone 2:** Budget-friendly, long standby, best for tropical and ocean routes.
- **Garmin inReach Mini 2:** Two-way text, GPS nav, compact.
- **Thuraya X5-Touch:** Android phone + satellite (not for N/S America).

Downsides: Subscription plans required, expensive bandwidth.

Ideal Users: Offshore sailors, bluewater cruisers, ocean kayakers.

AIS Man Overboard Beacon (Automatic Identification System)

Function: Sends an MOB distress signal via AIS to vessels within VHF range.

Activation: Manual or automatic (e.g., water-activated or with a life jacket tether).

What It Transmits:

- MMSI identifier.
- Precise GPS coordinates.
- Constant updates for drifting targets.

Benefits:

- Detectable by onboard chartplotters with AIS.
- High visibility to all vessels in range—not just SAR services.
- Seamless integration with marine electronics.

Design: Compact, waterproof, usually wearable.

Best For: MOB recovery in fleet races, sailing teams, solo mariners.

Signal Mirror

Operation: Reflects sunlight to visually signal rescuers or aircraft.

Mechanism:

- Aiming grid/sighting hole to direct sunlight.
- Bright flashes visible for miles in clear daylight.

Advantages:

- Lightweight and battery-free.
- Works in conjunction with other gear.
- Reliable backup for visual signaling.

Best Conditions: Clear, sunny weather.

Ideal Placement: Life jacket pocket or ditch bag.

Flares (Handheld, Parachute, Smoke)

Purpose: Used to visually signal distress during both day and night.

Types & Use Cases:

- **Handheld Flares:** Short-range, used to alert nearby vessels. Burn ~30–60 seconds.
- **Parachute Flares:** Launched sky-high (~300m), visible for miles, float slowly.
- **Smoke Flares:** Emit colored smoke for daytime location marking.

Critical Considerations:

- Keep dry and within expiry date.
- Store in waterproof, labeled container.
- Only use in genuine emergencies.

Complementary To: VHF, AIS, and satellite devices.

Navigation and Tracking Devices

GPS Device (Marine Handheld GPS)

Purpose: Pinpoints location using satellites; displays marine charts.

Primary Functions:

- Shows real-time position on screen.
- Saves waypoints, logs travel path.
- Enables route planning.

Best Features:

- Waterproof (IP67+).

- Long battery life; AA or rechargeable.
- High-resolution display.
- Can sync with PLBs or inReach units.

Emergency Benefits:
- Share coordinates during distress.
- Backtrack feature helps retrace route.
- Continuous location feed even without chartplotter.

Top Models: Garmin GPSMAP series, Garmin inReach Explorer+, Lowrance handhelds.

Survival and Emergency Power Devices

These ensure that critical electronics such as radios, GPS units, satellite phones, and beacons stay powered during extended emergencies.

Portable Solar Charger

Function: Converts sunlight into electricity using built-in solar panels.

Usage:
- Direct charging of devices via USB ports.
- Indirect charging of an integrated or external battery bank for use when the sun isn't shining.

Features:
- Wattage: Most marine-use panels are 5–15W; higher wattage = faster charge.
- Output Ports: USB-A, USB-C, sometimes DC barrel jacks.

- Smart Charging: Prevents overcharging; auto-adjusts to device needs.
- Waterproof or water-resistant construction (IP67+).

Ideal Use: Long offshore trips, dinghy expeditions, or coastal kayaking.

Power Bank

Function: Stores electrical energy to charge devices without real-time solar access.

Key Features:

- Capacity measured in mAh (10,000–20,000 mAh common for marine use).
- Can charge multiple devices simultaneously.
- Some models include built-in solar panel as a backup.
- Rugged, waterproof housing for marine environments.

Use Case: Keeps PLBs, radios, and phones powered in prolonged distress scenarios.

Hand-Crank or Solar-Powered Emergency Radio

Function: Receives NOAA weather alerts, news broadcasts, and emergency messages.

Key Benefits:

- Does not require standard batteries—runs on solar or crank power.
- Some models include USB charging ports for other devices.
- AM/FM + Weather band (NOAA) capable.

Why It's Important: Provides weather updates and alerts even in power outages or system failures.

First Aid and Survival Gear

These tools support injury treatment, hypothermia prevention, flotation, and signaling in extreme conditions.

Waterproof First Aid Kit

Design: Comes in a rugged, sealed container that protects against immersion, saltwater, and impact.

Key Contents:

- **Wound Care:** Waterproof bandages, gauze pads, medical tape, antiseptics.
- **Medications:** Pain relievers (aspirin, ibuprofen), antihistamines, seasickness pills.
- **Tools:** Stainless steel scissors, tweezers, gloves, splint materials.
- **Extras:** Burn gel, emergency blanket, CPR instructions.

Best Use: Essential for treating cuts, punctures, allergic reactions, burns, and hypothermia in wet environments.

Thermal Survival Blanket (Mylar Blanket)

Function: Reflects up to 90% of body heat back to the individual to reduce hypothermia risk.

Material: Lightweight, aluminized plastic (Mylar), highly reflective.

Uses:

- Personal warmth
- Wind break
- Ground insulator
- Visual signaling (can reflect light like a mirror)

Advantages: Ultra-compact, tear-resistant, waterproof, and extremely light.

Best Practice: Include one per person in ditch bag or life raft.

Personal Flotation Device (PFD) with Whistle & Light

Primary Purpose: Keeps wearer buoyant and visible in water, even if unconscious.

Core Components:

- High-buoyancy foam or CO_2 inflation system.
- Integrated whistle for audible signaling.
- Integrated waterproof strobe or LED light for night rescue.

Required Standards: Should meet USCG or SOLAS marine safety standards.

Why It's Crucial: Combines life-saving flotation with passive signaling features.

Pro Tip: Attach a PLB or AIS beacon directly to your PFD for best chance of detection.

Ditch Bags (Grab-and-Go Emergency Bags)

Designed to be grabbed during an emergency evacuation, ditch bags store essential equipment for survival, communication, and rescue coordination.

Ditch Bag (Floating and Waterproof)

Purpose: Organizes critical survival tools in one quickly accessible bag.

Design Features:

- Made from buoyant, durable material (often vinyl or PVC-coated nylon).
- Bright color (orange, red, or yellow) for high visibility.
- Sealed zippers or roll-top closures.
- Grab handles or shoulder straps.

Essential Contents Checklist:

- **PLB or EPIRB** – Core distress signaling.
- **Handheld VHF Radio** – Communication during rescue.
- **Waterproof Flashlight & Strobe Light** – Nighttime visibility.
- **Signal Mirror & Whistle** – Passive visual/auditory alerts.
- **Flares** – Visual emergency signals (multiple types).
- **Compass & Handheld GPS** – Navigation and position marking.
- **Water Pouches or Filtration Straw** – Clean drinking water supply.
- **High-Calorie Food Bars** – Compact emergency rations.

- **Waterproof First Aid Kit** – Wound care, medication, and protective gear.
- **Thermal Blanket** – Heat retention and shelter.
- **Multitool or Knife** – Versatile cutting, repair, or defense.
- **Duct Tape & Zip Ties** – For emergency repairs.
- **Fire Starter or Waterproof Matches** – If stranded on land.

Pro Tip: Store ditch bag in an unlocked compartment near the helm or emergency exit.

Ditch Bag Checklist for Marine Emergency Preparedness

Communication & Signaling:

- **PLB or EPIRB** – Personal locator or vessel beacon for satellite rescue
- **Handheld VHF Marine Radio** – Waterproof, floating, with DSC if possible
- **Waterproof Flashlight & Strobe Light** – Nighttime visibility
- **Signal Mirror & Whistle** – Daytime and auditory alert tools
- **Flares** – Handheld, parachute, and/or smoke (check expiration)

Navigation Tools:

- **Compass (Marine Grade, Liquid-Filled)** – Analog backup to GPS
- **Handheld GPS Unit** – For accurate location and waypoint tracking

Hydration & Food:

- **Water Pouches (Coast Guard approved)** or **Filtration Straw**
- **High-Calorie Emergency Food Bars** – Long shelf life, compact

First Aid & Medical:

- **Waterproof First Aid Kit** – Bandages, meds, antiseptic, gloves, seasickness tablets

Survival Gear:

- **Thermal Blanket (Mylar)** – Heat retention, wind/rain shelter
- **Multitool or Marine Knife** – Versatile cutting, survival tool
- **Duct Tape & Zip Ties** – Quick repairs and gear bundling
- **Fire Starter or Waterproof Matches** – Emergency fire-starting tool

Final Summary

Each of these devices serves a specific survival function:

- **Signaling & Rescue:** EPIRBs, PLBs, VHF radios, satellite phones, AIS beacons.
- **Navigation & Tracking:** GPS devices, compasses.
- **Power Supply:** Solar chargers, power banks, crank radios.
- **Survival:** First aid kits, PFDs, blankets, mirrors, ditch bags.

A properly equipped vessel should have **redundancy**, with **at least two layers of signaling, navigation, and survival gear**. The ditch bag should be the final fallback when abandoning ship.

Chapter 57

COAST GUARD PROCEDURES

Initial Assessment

Evaluate the emergency (medical, fire, sinking), ensure passenger safety, gather key details (location, nature of emergency, vessel info).

Contacting Rescue Services Using a Marine VHF

Channel 16 – Distress/hailing frequency; always monitored.

Distress Call (MAYDAY)

- "MAYDAY" x 3 + vessel name + position + nature of emergency + number of people onboard.
- Wait for response and follow instructions.

Urgent but Non-Life-Threatening Situations (PAN-PAN)

- For non-life-threatening issues (e.g., engine failure).

Safety Information (SECURITÉ)

- For navigational warnings or weather updates.

Contacting the Coast Guard Using a Digital Selective Calling (DSC) Radio

DSC Radio Feature

- Press and hold DISTRESS button (~5 seconds) for automated digital alert with GPS position.
- Coast Guard will acknowledge; follow up with a voice transmission.

Other Communication Methods

Mobile Phones

- Dial 911 (if in range) or *CG in some regions, though coverage may be limited offshore.

Satellite Phones

- Useful offshore; direct contact with rescue services.

EPIRB

- Emergency Position Indicating Radio Beacon—sends vessel info and location via satellite.

Key Information to Provide

- Vessel name, location (coordinates), nature of emergency, assistance required, people onboard, vessel description.

Staying Safe While Awaiting Rescue

- Distribute life jackets, minimize vessel movement, use flares/flags/lights to remain visible, keep radio on Channel 16.

Post-Emergency Follow-Up

- Document incident details, check and restock emergency supplies, report to authorities or insurance as needed.

Chapter 58

CONTACTING RESCUE SERVICES AND COORDINATING WITH NEARBY VESSELS

Establishing Contact with Nearby Vessels

Using VHF Marine Radio

- Select Channel 16 (international distress/hailing).
- Transmit "PAN-PAN" or "MAYDAY" (severity-based).
- Provide vessel name, location, nature of emergency, and requested assistance.
- Acknowledge and confirm any responses received.

Using Digital Selective Calling (DSC)

- Activate DSC to broadcast automated distress alerts, then follow up on Channel 16.

Using Audible or Visual Signals

- Flares, sound signals, or hand gestures for attracting attention if radio fails or visibility is poor.

Coordinating Rescue Efforts with Nearby Vessels

Identify Responding Vessels

- Confirm their identity, location, and estimated time of arrival (ETA).

Assign Roles and Responsibilities

- Designate a lead vessel (if multiple respond).
- Assign tasks such as towing, medical aid, or passenger transfer.

Share Information

- Update on emergency details (e.g., people onboard, vessel condition).
- Agree on a working radio channel (keeping Channel 16 open).

Navigation and Approach

- Provide safe approach zones.
- Instruct rescuers on which side to approach to avoid further damage.

Providing Assistance

On-Site Support

- Towing: Secure lines, ensure towing vessel can handle the load.
- Medical Aid: Transfer injured to responding vessel if needed.
- Passenger Transfer: Use life rafts or safe boarding procedures.

Monitoring and Reporting

- Maintain continuous communication to update all involved on the situation (e.g., "Under tow, heading to nearest harbor").

Key Points to Communicate

- Situation updates (any change in emergency status).
- Weather and sea conditions.
- Rescue plan details (destination, timeline, expected arrival).

Post-Rescue Actions

Express Gratitude

- Acknowledge and thank assisting vessels over the radio.

Report the Incident

- Notify maritime authorities and file an official report if needed.

Inspect and Restock Equipment

- Replace used flares, first aid supplies, and verify rescue equipment integrity.

Best Practices for Coordinating with Nearby Vessels

- Stay calm and communicate clearly.
- Use standard maritime language (avoiding slang).
- Prioritize safety and stabilize conditions before action.
- Keep radios on and all responding parties updated.

Conclusion

- Effective coordination with nearby vessels greatly increases rescue success.
- Clear communication, role assignment, and maritime protocol adherence are key.

Chapter 59

WHAT TO EXPECT DURING
A RESCUE OPERATION

Initial Response

Confirmation of Distress Call

- Expect acknowledgment from Coast Guard or nearby vessels.
- Provide additional requested info (position, emergency type, people onboard).

Reassurance and Communication

- Rescuers confirm help is en route, give instructions (monitor Channel 16).

Arrival of Assistance

Rescue Vessel or Aircraft

- May include Coast Guard ships, helicopters, or private/commercial vessels.

- They might use visual signals (lights, flares) or loudspeakers to identify themselves.

Identification and Positioning

- Rescue units verify your vessel by name, color, or type.
- You might use flares/flags to guide them.

Approach

- Rescuers approach cautiously to avoid collision or further harm.
- Aircraft may lower personnel or supplies from above.

Rescue Procedures

Stabilization of the Emergency

- Deployment of life rafts, life jackets, or pumps for water ingress.
- Fire suppression, if necessary.

Evacuation

- Injured or vulnerable passengers evacuated first.
- Methods: Transfer to rescue vessel via ladder/raft or helicopter hoist.
- Follow rescuer instructions for orderly evacuation.

Communication During Rescue

Constant Updates

- Provide ongoing info on vessel status or changes in conditions.

Instructions from Rescuers

- Prepare for towing or gather passengers in specific areas.
- Abandon ship if directed.

Rescue Challenges

Weather and Sea Conditions

- High winds, rough seas, or storms may complicate rescue.

Limited Visibility

- Nighttime or fog necessitates extra signals (strobe lights, flares).

Crew and Passenger Cooperation

- Calmness and adherence to directions ensure safer, faster rescue.

Post-Rescue Actions

Transportation to Safety

- Rescuers bring you to nearest port or medical facility if required.

Retrieval of Vessel

- If salvageable, it may be towed; if lost, authorities are notified.

Reporting and Documentation

- Expect to give a detailed account of the incident for official records.

Psychological Impact

- Relief and possible shock are common.
- A post-rescue debriefing may occur to ensure all are accounted for and calm.

Key Tips to Remember During Rescue

- Stay calm to avoid panic.
- Follow rescuers' instructions carefully.
- Prepare for evacuation (life jackets, essential items).
- Keep communication equipment powered and ready.
- Secure valuables and documents if time allows.

Conclusion

- A maritime rescue demands cooperation, clear communication, and following protocols.
- Understanding the process and maintaining composure can greatly improve safety and outcomes.

PART TEN

TAKING ON WATER

CRASH PUMP OVERVIEW

Bilge Versus Crash Pumps

Definition of a Crash Pump

- High-capacity pump designed for rapid water removal during flooding.

Purpose

- Handles large volumes quickly in emergencies (breaches, leaks, severe weather).

Comparison to Standard Bilge Pumps

- Crash pumps have a much higher flow rate (GPM vs. GPH focus).
- Standard bilge pumps suffice for routine water removal but are inadequate for large-scale flooding.

Types of Crash Pumps & Support Systems

Engine-Driven Crash Pumps

- Powered by the boat's main or auxiliary engine; high capacity (hundreds of GPM).

Electric Crash Pumps

- Boat's electrical system (12V or 24V); requires robust wiring and power backup.

Portable Crash Pumps

- Self-contained (gas, diesel, battery); can be deployed anywhere on the vessel.

Manual Crash Pumps

- Operated by hand or foot; last-resort when power/fuel are unavailable.

Support Systems

- Power Supply
- Adequate batteries, engine maintenance, or fuel reserves.
- Intake & Discharge Hoses
- Durable hoses and strainers to manage debris.
- Bilge Layout
- Compartmentalization for efficient water collection.
- Monitoring Systems
- High-water alarms, flow indicators, float switches.
- Crew Training
- Everyone should know how to deploy and operate crash pumps.

Seeking Help Setting Up a Crash Pump

Marine Electricians

- Ensure proper wiring, breakers, grounding.

Marine Mechanics

- Install engine-driven pumps or ensure correct mechanical connections.

Boat Builders/Shipyards

- Retrofit hull for fittings, mounts, and reinforcements.

Marine Surveyors

- Recommend appropriate pump type and check compliance.

Specialized Equipment Dealers

- Advise on selecting the right pump based on boat specs.

Electrical Output: 12V vs. 24V

- 12V Common for small/medium vessels, easy parts availability.
- 24V Common on larger vessels, more efficient for high-capacity pumps.
- Compatibility crucial (pumps must match boat's voltage).

Additional Installation Considerations

Power Management

- Dedicated switches/fuses, marine-grade wiring.

Redundancy

- Backup manual or portable pumps.

Regular Testing

- Simulate emergency pumping to confirm readiness.

Ease of Using Crash Pumps on Boats with Electric Reels

Medium/Large Fishing Boats

- Often have a 12V system for electric reels; adding a 12V crash pump is straightforward.

24V Systems

- More common on larger vessels or high-powered reels; crash pumps also available in 24V.

Compatibility

- Check reel/pump voltage and use DC-DC converters if needed.

Chapter **61**

COMMON SCENARIOS FOR WATER BREACH

When a boat suffers a **hull breach**, the decision to attempt repair or **abandon ship** depends on several interrelated factors:

- **Breach size**
- **Breach location**
- **Sea conditions**
- **Availability of tools and repair materials**
- **Pump capacity**
- **Remaining structural integrity of the vessel**

This section offers a structured analysis based on **breach severity**:

Hull Breach Size and Reparability

Small Breaches (Under 1–2 inches in diameter)

Examples:

- A screw or bolt pulled loose from a fitting

- Cracks or punctures from floating debris
- A hull breach caused by a boat hook, tool, or grounding on coral/rock

Reparability Tactics:

Wooden Plugs (Tapered Bungs):
- Jammed into through-hull holes or pipe breaches
- Swell when wet, improving the seal

Epoxy Sticks or Marine Putty:
- Can be applied underwater
- Good for small cracks, seams, or punctures

Fiberglass Tape or Patch:
- Used with resin to reinforce small cracks

Duct Tape or Rubber Sheeting:
- Used in calm water for above-waterline leaks as a short-term patch

Bilge Pumps:
- Effective at keeping up with minor water ingress
- Monitor flow rate to confirm stability

Crew Can Manage with Minimal Tools and No External Assistance

Decision: Proceed with on-board repairs and monitor. No need to abandon ship unless the breach expands or conditions worsen

Medium Breaches (2–12 inches in diameter)

Examples:

- Collision with semi-submerged objects (e.g., logs or containers)
- Ramming a dock or piling
- Failed seacock or through-hull fitting blown out
- Compromised exhaust outlet or rudder post seal

Reparability Tactics:

Plywood or Sailcloth Patches:

- Custom cut and applied over breach using bolts, screws, or lashing
- Secured inside or outside hull depending on access

Underwater Epoxy Putty or Marine Sealant:

- For sealing below-waterline breaches
- Use putty sticks in urgent cases; combine with external reinforcement

Compression from the Inside:

- Place patch, board, or brace over inner hull wall
- Secure with battens and tiedown straps to create back pressure

Use of Crash Pumps or High-Capacity Bilge Pumps:

- Must outpace incoming water
- If not, repair is unsustainable

Crew Roles Must Be Assigned:

- One to apply pressure
- One to operate pumps
- One to monitor ingress rate and hull flex

Decision:

- If pumps can keep up and the patch holds, continue repairs.
- If ingress increases or structure worsens, prepare to abandon ship.

Large Breaches (Over 12 inches or multiple feet)

Examples:

- Collision with a shipping container or another vessel
- Hull cracked open from severe grounding
- Hull failure due to rot, rust, or delamination
- Keel separation or major impact below the waterline

Reparability Tactics:

Collision Mats or External Tarps:

- Deploy over the side, anchored or tied tightly
- Water pressure helps hold the mat to the hull
- Interior bracing may be needed for full seal

Use of Multiple Layers:

- First layer provides immediate cover
- Additional tarps or mats improve sealing and durability

Crew Coordination Required:

- One team on deck to deploy and position
- One team inside to brace or patch

Crash Pumps or Multiple Bilge Pumps:

- Critical to slow rising water
- Check voltage and battery state if pumps begin to lose flow

Sealant or Epoxy Edging:
- Apply around tarp/mat edges to reduce water seepage

Weight Redistribution:
- Move cargo, gear, or personnel to stabilize boat and reduce strain on breached side

Decision Factors:
- If breach grows despite efforts, prepare for immediate evacuation

If bilge pump capacity is overwhelmed, **issue MAYDAY** and begin abandon ship protocol
- Crew safety takes priority over saving the vessel

Breach Summary Table (At-a-Glance)

Breach Type	Size	Repair Method	Pump Needed	Evac Risk
Small	< 2 inches	Plugs, epoxy, tape	Standard bilge pump	Low
Medium	2–12 inches	Plywood patch, epoxy, brace system	High-capacity pump	Moderate
Large	> 12 inches	Tarps, collision mats, crash pump support	Multiple crash pumps	High or Critical

Hull Breach Size and Reparability

Small Breaches (1–2 inches)

- Potentially fixable with wooden plugs, epoxy, or minor patches.
- Bilge pumps can manage minimal water ingress.

Medium Breaches (2–12 inches)

- May require plywood patches, sailcloth, or underwater epoxy.
- Bilge pumps must handle moderate flow; calm conditions help.

Large Breaches (Over 12 inches)

- Can involve collision mats, tarps, or major structural patches.
- High-capacity pumps are crucial; repairs often temporary.

Tarps/Collision Mats

Exterior Application

- Lower tarp overboard, secure with ropes so water pressure helps seal.

Interior Application

- Brace tarp/mat from the inside with battens or boards.

Reinforcement

- Seal edges with epoxy or sealant; add layers if needed.

Limitations

- Temporary measure for large breaches; rough seas can dislodge material.

Factors to Consider Before Abandoning Ship

Rate of Water Ingress

- Exceeds pumping capacity $\Rightarrow$ potential abandonment.

Structural Integrity

- Severe hull damage or listing is a critical risk factor.

Location of Breach

- Lower or deeper breaches usually worse.

Weather & Sea Conditions

- Rough seas escalate damage and hamper repairs.

Available Resources

- Tools, materials, and experienced crew improve survival chances.

Communication & Rescue Options

- Far from help might require staying aboard longer; use radios, EPIRBs, flares.

When to Call "Abandon Ship"

- Immediate danger (sinking/capsizing).
- No hope of repair; structural failure imminent.
- Environmental hazards (fire, storms, rocks).
- Confirm readiness with authorities (MAYDAY, rescue coordination).

Assessing & Repair of Water Breach

Structural Damage

Hull Breach

- Collision, grounding, debris impacts.

Emergency Fixes

- Plug or patch (e.g., epoxy, collision mat); monitor via pumps.

Wooden Plugs

Sizes/Shapes

- Tapered, various diameters (½–3 inch at wide end).

Installation

- Hammer/force plug into hole; secure with tape/cloth/epoxy.

Limits

- Best for small to medium leaks.
- High pressure or large holes may overwhelm plugs.

Marine Epoxies for Hull Breach Repair

Types of Marine Epoxies

Two-Part Epoxies

- Resin + hardener mixed before use; very strong and durable.

- Ideal for larger or more critical repairs; requires correct mixing and curing time.

Putty or Stick Epoxies

- pre-mixed, clay-like sticks for quick fixes.
- Can be applied underwater or in damp conditions; not as strong as two-part mixes.

Sizes and Packaging

- Two-Part: Sold in cans/tubes (4 oz to 1 gallon).
- Epoxy Sticks: Typically 3–12 inches in length, ~1 inch diameter.

Installation Steps

Preparation

- Clean the breach area; remove grease/debris.
- Dry if possible (some epoxies can bond when wet).

Mix (Two-Part Only)

- Combine resin and hardener thoroughly (often 1:1 ratio).

Application

- Spread or press epoxy firmly over/into the breach.
- Mold to match hull contours; ensure full coverage.

Curing

- Follow manufacturer's recommended cure times (minutes to hours).
- Minimize boat movement during curing.

Limits of Marine Epoxies

Size of the Breach

- Effective for small-to-medium holes (~up to 2–3 inches).
- Large breaches may require reinforcement (fiberglass, patches).

Pressure Resistance

- Handles moderate water pressure; extreme pressure may overwhelm it.

Application Conditions

- Some epoxies can be applied underwater; others need dry surfaces.

Temporary Nature

- Usually a stopgap measure until permanent repair can be done.

Best Practices

- Carry both two-part epoxies and epoxy sticks on board.
- Practice during non-emergency times to learn mixing/ application.
- Reinforce large or irregular breaches with cloth, tape, or wooden patches.
- Check the epoxy repair frequently—especially if it's holding back water.

Fiberglass Patches for Hull Breach Repair

Types of Fiberglass Patches

Fiberglass Cloth

- Woven, flexible; good for curved surfaces and layering.
- Available in different weights (e.g., 10 oz, 14 oz).

Fiberglass Mat

- Non-woven, thicker, adds bulk and strength.
- Often combined with fiberglass cloth for multi-layer repairs.

Pre-Cut Fiberglass Patches

- Ready-made, sometimes pre-saturated with resin.

Sizes and Shapes

- Sheets range from small squares (a few inches) to large rolls (several feet wide).
- Easily cut with scissors to fit breach dimensions.

Installation Steps

Preparation

- Sand and clean the area; remove debris, grease, or loose paint.

Cut the Patch

- Ensure patch extends ~2–4 inches beyond the breach edges.

Mix Resin

- Follow resin/hardener instructions precisely.

Apply the Patch

- Brush resin onto the hull, lay the fiberglass, then saturate it with more resin.
- Roll or squeegee out air bubbles; layer multiple patches if needed.

Curing

- Allow several hours (or per product guidelines) for full cure.
- Avoid water exposure or vessel movement during curing.

Limits of Fiberglass Patches

Size of the Breach

- Effective for small-to-medium (up to ~12 inches).
- Larger breaches may need reinforcement (plywood, tarps).

Application Conditions

- Generally best in dry conditions unless using special underwater resin.

Temporary vs. Permanent

- Can be a strong, lasting repair if properly layered and cured.

Skill and Time

- Requires some know-how; curing time may be an issue during active flooding.

Best Practices

- Keep a fiberglass repair kit (cloth/mat, resin, hardener) on board.

- Reinforce large breaches with extra layers, collision mats, or epoxy.
- Sand and finish the patch for a smoother, more permanent seal if time allows.

Preventive Measures

- Regular Inspection
- Check hull integrity, through-hulls, fittings.
- Maintain bilge and crash pumps.
- Keep an emergency repair kit (plugs, epoxy, collision mats, tarps).
- Conduct drills for patching breaches and deploying pumps.

Mechanical Failures & Temporary Sealing Compounds

Leaking Propeller Shaft

- Common causes: Worn seals/bearings.

Temporary Fixes

- Marine epoxy putty (knead and press around the seal).
- Silicone sealant (fast, flexible).
- Self-fusing silicone tape (wrap around shaft area).
- Underwater epoxy if leak is below the waterline.
- Adjust packing nuts on a stuffing box if applicable.

Failed Through-Hull Fittings

- Causes: Corrosion, age, improper installation.
- Carry spare fittings, sealing compound.
- Close seacocks when not in use; replace damaged fittings ASAP.

Cooling System Leaks

- Cracked hoses, loose clamps, corroded parts.
- Regular inspection; replace failing components.
- Watch engine temp gauges for early warning.

Weather, Human Error & Wear

Heavy Rain / Storms

- Ensure hatches/ports are sealed.
- Use high-capacity pumps to manage water influx.
- Secure items on deck to prevent wave overwash.

Human Errors

- Open hatches, overloading—double-check weight distribution and closures.

Equipment Failures

- Bilge pump malfunctions (blockages, electrical failures).
- Battery or wiring issues (corrosion, drained battery).
- Always carry backup pumps or manual pumping options.

Preventive Measures & Maintenance

Regular Maintenance

Small Boat Checklist

- Engine/fuel system checks, prop/steering inspection.
- Hull integrity, drain plugs, deck hardware.
- Safety gear (life jackets, flares, first aid).

- Test bilge pump, radio, and navigation lights.

Large Boat Checklist

- Engines (oil, belts, coolant), fuel tanks, generators.
- Through-hull fittings, hull anti-fouling, rudder/steering.
- Life rafts, EPIRBs, flares, fire extinguishers.
- Electronics (radar, GPS, AIS), bilge pumps, black/greywater systems.
- Secure cargo and run sea trials.

Key Takeaways

- Marine epoxy and fiberglass patches provide **essential** emergency hull repair options, each with its **own limitations**.
- **Mechanical failures** (leaking shafts, fittings) can be temporarily mitigated with quick-fix compounds until proper repairs.
- **Preventive maintenance** (routine checks, thorough checklists) significantly reduces risk and ensures readiness.
- Always carry **redundant repair supplies** (epoxy, fiberglass cloth, plugs) and **test** them during non-emergency times.
- Proper **safety gear** and **emergency procedures** are critical for handling flooding or hull breaches effectively.

Emergency Equipment Checklist

Small Boats

- Life jackets, throwable device, fire extinguisher, flares.
- Handheld VHF, compass, flashlight, wooden plugs.
- Manual bilge pump, spare ropes/lines.

Large Boats

- Life jackets/rafts, EPIRB, multiple fire extinguishers.
- Fixed/handheld VHF with DSC, radar reflector.
- Expanded tool kit (spare parts, patch kit, epoxy).
- Ample water, rations, backup batteries.

Anchoring and Mooring

Primary Anchor with Adequate Chain and Rode

- Essential for secure anchorage in various seabeds.
- Chain or rode length should be sufficient for expected depths and weather conditions.

Secondary Anchor (for Emergencies)

- Backup if the primary anchor drags or for setting a second anchor in strong winds/currents.

Mooring Lines and Extra Fenders

- High-quality ropes sized appropriately for boat length and weight.
- Multiple fenders for protection when docking or rafted to other vessels.

Additional Large Boat-Specific Items

Collision Mats (For Large Hull Breaches)

- Heavy-duty mats or tarps to temporarily seal hull breaches from the outside.

Heavy-Duty Tow Line

- Capable of handling the vessel's tonnage in case of breakdown or rescue assistance.

Underwater Repair Tools

- Patches, tarps, underwater epoxy for on-the-spot repairs below the waterline.

Portable Generator

- Provides backup power for pumps, communication, and essential systems if main power fails.

Life Sling / Man Overboard Recovery System

- Specialized gear to assist in recovering an overboard crew member.

Weather Monitoring System or Barometer

- Helps track changes in atmospheric pressure and weather patterns for safer navigation.

General Maintenance Notes

1. Regularly Inspect & Replace

- Check all emergency and safety gear for damage or expiration (flares, fire extinguishers, epoxies, etc.).

2. Crew Familiarity

- Ensure all passengers/crew know where emergency equipment is stored and how to use it.

3. Pre-Departure Testing

- Confirm communication devices (VHF, satellite phone) and navigation aids (GPS, radar) are functioning properly.

Safety Drills for Crew

Safety Drills for a Small Boat

1. Man Overboard (MOB) Drill

- Spotter keeps visual contact; practice quick-turn approach and use of flotation devices.

2. Fire Drill

- Identify fire source; practice using extinguishers and ventilation/shutdown procedures.

3. Emergency Stop Drill

- Learn to cut engine or fuel supply; simulate emergency anchor deployment.

4. Abandon Ship Drill

- Don life jackets; deploy dinghy/life raft; practice flares or VHF distress signals.

5. Navigation Emergency Drill

- Practice backup navigation (compass, paper charts) if GPS fails; coordinate with Coast Guard or nearby boats.

Safety Drills for a Large Boat

1. Man Overboard Drill

- Use life rings or specialized retrieval (life sling, hoist); monthly frequency recommended.

2. Fire Drill

- Assign firefighting and communication roles; simulate using extinguishers and isolating affected areas.

3. Abandon Ship Drill

- Conduct roll call, don life jackets/immersion suits; practice launching life rafts and using EPIRB.

4. Collision / Hull Breach Drill

- Deploy collision mats, use crash pumps, and simulate sealing a breach.

5. Medical Emergency Drill

- Practice first aid, CPR, and contacting medevac or Coast Guard.

6. Navigation & Communication Drill

- Use backup systems (paper charts, handheld radios) if primary systems fail.

7. Man Overboard Recovery Using Hoists

- Practice lifting an incapacitated person from the water with a davit system.

Best Practices for Safety Drills

- Document drills in a logbook (date, participants, outcomes).
- Debrief afterward—note improvements needed.
- Rotate crew roles for comprehensive training.
- Simulate realistic conditions (use actual equipment, alarms, etc.).
- Conduct drills regularly per vessel type and regulations.

Chapter 62

EMERGENCY PROCEDURES

Steps for Assessing Water Ingress

1. Stay Calm & Alert Crew

- Announce potential flooding; assign roles (observation, pumping, communication).

2. Locate the Leak

- Check hull for cracks, through-hull fittings, shaft seals, deck hatches, and plumbing lines.

3. Assess Severity

- Estimate water accumulation rate; evaluate structural damage.

4. Identify Affected Areas

- Which compartments are flooding? Check electrical systems for submersion risk.

5. Determine Repair Accessibility

- Decide if you can patch or plug the leak (wooden plugs, epoxy, collision mats).

6. Activate Emergency Measures

- Start bilge/crash pumps; seal the leak with temporary methods.

7. Monitor Continuously

- Track water levels, check if repair is holding.

8. Decide Next Steps

- If controllable, head for nearest port. If not, prepare for abandon ship and call for help.

How to Activate Emergency Response Systems

1. Assess the Situation

- Identify the nature (fire, flooding, engine failure) and severity of emergency.

2. Alert the Crew

- Sound alarms or use PA; assign emergency roles.

3. Broadcast a Distress Signal

- **VHF Channel 16** for "MAYDAY" (life-threatening) or "PAN-PAN" (urgent but not immediately life-threatening).
- Provide vessel name, position, nature of emergency, number of people.

4. Activate Internal Systems

- Run bilge/crash pumps, use fire extinguishers, etc.

5. Contact Authorities

- Call the Coast Guard or local SAR (Search and Rescue) coordination center.
- Use EPIRB if in severe distress or out of radio range.

6. Coordinate with Nearby Vessels

- Request immediate help on VHF; share location and problem details.

7. Follow Emergency Procedures

- Distribute life jackets, ready life rafts, secure loose items.

8. Key Contacts

- Coast Guard numbers, SAR centers, vessel maintenance providers.
- Pre-program these in radios/phones.

Communication Protocols with Rescue Authorities

Preparing to Abandon Ship

- MAYDAY on Channel 16; repeat vessel info, position, nature of emergency.
- Activate EPIRB, deploy flares, ensure crew dons life jackets.

Managing a Boating Emergency (No Abandon Ship Yet)

- Assess severity; use "PAN-PAN" if non-life-threatening.
- Keep radio on Channel 16; provide regular updates.

Post-Communication Actions

- Stay calm; follow instructions from Coast Guard/SAR.
- Maintain visibility (lights, flares) if nighttime or poor visibility.

Key Points to Provide

- Vessel name/call sign, position, type of emergency, number of people onboard, any special needs.

Who to Contact

- Coast Guard (Channel 16, local phone).
- Search and Rescue Centers (regional or national numbers).
- Nearby vessels (VHF hailing).

Best Practices

- Pre-program channels & phone numbers.
- Practice communication drills; log all radio calls.
- Prepare a grab bag (ID, flares, first aid, communication devices) if evacuation is imminent.

Key Takeaways

- Proper **anchoring/mooring gear** and **large boat-specific items** (collision mats, heavy tow lines) greatly enhance preparedness.
- **Regular maintenance checks** and **crew familiarity** with safety gear are crucial for quick response.
- **Safety drills** (man overboard, fire, abandon ship, hull breach) should be routine for both small and large vessels.
- **Water ingress** assessment involves calm, methodical steps: locate leak, estimate severity, seal if possible, and monitor.

- **Emergency activation** (MAYDAY, EPIRB, contacting authorities) must be conducted in a structured way—everyone onboard should know the protocol.
- **Communication** with rescue agencies must be clear, complete, and regularly updated to ensure effective assistance.

Conclusion: Importance of Preparation for a Water Breach

1. Prevents Catastrophic Damage

- **Minimizes Flooding**: Quick action (bilge pumps, sealing the breach) reduces water ingress and risk of sinking.
- **Protects Critical Systems**: Early detection safeguards engines, electrical systems, and navigation tools.

2. Ensures Crew and Passenger Safety

- **Avoids Panic**: A prepared crew acts calmly and reduces injury risk.
- **Supports Evacuation**: Life rafts, jackets, and other safety gear must be ready for immediate use.

3. Improves Response Time

- **Quick Repairs**: Tools like wooden plugs, tarps, epoxy enable rapid sealing.
- **Efficient Communication**: Trained crew can send a MAYDAY or activate EPIRB swiftly.

4. Enhances Vessel Stability

- **Prevents Capsizing**: Fast response maintains buoyancy and balance.

- **Reduces Weight Shift**: Proper water management avoids dangerous listing.

5. Meets Regulatory and Safety Standards

- **Compliance**: Authorities require specific gear and drills.
- **Insurance**: Preparedness demonstrates due diligence and can affect claims.

6. Reduces Long-Term Costs

- **Prevents Extensive Repairs**: Minimizes damage, lowering repair bills.
- **Avoids Salvage Expenses**: Proper readiness reduces total-loss scenarios and salvage fees.

7. Boosts Confidence in Handling Emergencies

- **Trained Crew**: Regular drills ensure everyone knows their role.
- **Passenger Reassurance**: Visible preparedness instills trust.

8. Protects the Environment

- **Prevents Fuel Spills**: Controlling water ingress limits leaks of hazardous materials.
- **Minimizes Pollution**: Proper measures lower the risk of environmental harm.

How to Prepare for a Water Breach

- **Carry Emergency Repair Tools** (plugs, epoxy, collision mats, bilge pumps).
- **Regular Inspections** (hull integrity, through-hulls, seals).

- **Conduct Safety Drills** (hull breach response, communicating with rescue authorities).
- **Install Emergency Systems** (high-capacity bilge pumps, EPIRBs, backup power).
- **Create a Contingency Plan** (assign crew roles, outline steps for breach response).

Conclusion

Preparation for a water breach involves having the right **tools**, **training**, and **vessel maintenance** routines to protect lives, property, and the environment. It's about **acting swiftly and efficiently** when emergencies strike.

Summary of Best Practices for Boating Safety and Emergency Preparedness

1. Regular Maintenance and Inspections

- Check hull, through-hull fittings, bilge pumps, and electrical systems.
- Ensure safety gear is in good condition and properly stowed.

2. Emergency Preparedness

- Store essential repair items: wooden plugs, epoxy, collision mats, duct tape.
- Familiarize all crew with the location and operation of life jackets, fire extinguishers, EPIRBs.

3. Training and Drills

- Conduct drills for man overboard, fire response, hull breach, abandoning ship.

- Practice communication protocols (distress calls, navigation tools).

4. Effective Communication

- Use VHF Channel 16 for emergencies; know how to send MAYDAY or Pan-Pan.
- Maintain clarity and calmness when coordinating with rescue authorities or nearby vessels.

5. Rapid Response to Emergencies

- Immediately locate and assess any water ingress.
- Use available resources (plugs, collision mats, pumps) to mitigate flooding or damage.

6. Carry Redundant Systems

- Backup bilge pumps, extra power supplies, spare navigation tools.
- Ensure duplicates of critical safety equipment (handheld VHF, batteries).

7. Safety Equipment Readiness

- Keep life rafts, flares, rations, and first-aid kits accessible.
- Check expiration dates (flares, fire extinguishers, medical supplies).

8. Environmental Awareness

- Monitor weather forecasts before/during trips.
- Prepare for possible rough seas or cold water conditions.

9. Documentation and Logs

- Record maintenance, inspections, and drill sessions.
- Keep emergency contacts and communication guides in an easy-to-find place.

10. Calm and Coordinated Actions

- Assign clear roles to crew; keep situational awareness high.
- Adapt actions as conditions evolve—never let panic override procedure.

By following these best practices, boaters **significantly increase** the safety and resilience of both crew and vessel, ensuring prompt and effective responses to emergencies.

PART ELEVEN

SURVIVAL SITUATIONS

CHAPTER 63

WHEN TO MAKE THE DECISION TO ABANDON SHIP

General Principle: Stay With the Ship

- Vessel usually offers more shelter/visibility than a raft.
- Only abandon if remaining onboard poses imminent danger.

Factors to Consider

Condition of Vessel

- Flooding, sinking, uncontrollable fire, or structural failure.

Environmental Conditions

- Weather severity, proximity to rescue, water temperature.

Survival Equipment

- Availability of life rafts, life jackets, communication devices.

Crew/Passenger Condition

- Medical emergencies, injuries, readiness to evacuate.

Key Indicators for Abandonment

- Imminent sinking or submersion.
- Uncontrollable fire or explosion risk.
- Severe structural failure compromising safety.
- Inability to communicate or call for help while situation worsens.

Preparing to Abandon Ship

Issue the Order

- Captain/lead announces clearly, uses alarms, instructions.

Equip All Passengers

- Life jackets, emergency rations, flares, EPIRBs, radios.

Deploy Life Rafts

- Inflate/secure rafts, check functionality.

Secure Communication

- Activate EPIRBs, maintain radio contact if possible.

Steps to Safely Abandon Ship

- Orderly boarding, avoid overloading rafts.
- Perform headcount, activate survival gear.
- Move away from sinking vessel.
- Conserve supplies and watch for rescuers.

Psychological Preparedness

- Stay calm, reassure crew/passengers, remain vigilant.
- Avoid premature abandonment or ignoring critical equipment.

CHAPTER 64

DEPLOYING AND USING LIFE RAFTS

When to Deploy Life Rafts

- Only when remaining on vessel becomes more dangerous than leaving.
- Indicators: Severe flooding, uncontrollable fire, major structural damage.

Preparation

Check Readiness

- Inspect life rafts, safety seals, gather emergency supplies.

Choose Deployment Location

- Leeward side to minimize wind/wave impact, ensure area is clear of fire/debris.

Deployment Procedure

Launch the Raft

- Secure painter line, throw container overboard, pull to inflate.

Boarding

- One at a time, use ladders/ropes, assist injured/weak.

Detach from Vessel

- Cut or release painter line once everyone is safely aboard.

Using Life Rafts Safely

Organize the Raft

- Headcount, assign tasks, close canopy.

Resource Management

- Ration food/water, use flares/EPIRB for rescue signaling.

Maintain Stability

- Avoid overloading, distribute weight, use sea anchor if needed.

Communication

- Monitor rescue channels on handheld VHF if available.

Safety Tips

Stay Together

- Tether multiple rafts, share resources.

Monitor Environment

- Move away from sinking vessel, avoid collisions.

Watch for Rescuers

- Use signals (flares, mirrors) to attract attention.

Chapter 65

THE ESSENTIALS TO TAKE WITH YOU

Personal Safety Equipment

Life Jackets
- Mandatory for flotation and visibility.

Survival Suits (if available)
- Protect against cold water/hypothermia.

Safety Harness
- Prevents falling overboard during transition.

Communication & Signaling Devices

EPIRB
- Transmits location to rescue services.

Handheld VHF Radio
- Enables direct communication with rescuers/ nearby vessels.

Flares & Smoke Signals

- Attract attention day or night.

Flashlights/Strobe Lights

- Enhance visibility in low-light conditions.

Whistle or Horn

- Audible distress signal.

Navigation Tools

Compass

- Basic orientation if drifting.

Signal Mirror

- Reflects sunlight to alert distant rescuers.

First Aid Supplies

First Aid Kit

- Bandages, antiseptics, pain relievers, etc.

Seasickness Tablets

- Reduces nausea, dehydration risk.

Survival Gear

Knife or Multi-Tool

- Cutting lines, opening supplies, etc.

Waterproof Matches/Lighter

- Fire-starting for warmth/signaling post-rescue.

Thermal Blankets

- Retain body heat.

Sea Anchor (Drogue)

- Stabilizes raft, slows drifting.

Food & Water

Emergency Rations

- High-energy, non-perishable.

Drinking Water

- At least 1 liter/person/day.

Water Purification Tablets

- Treat potentially contaminated water.

Shelter/Protection

Canopy or Tarp

- Shields from sun, rain, wind.

Sunscreen & Sunglasses

- Prevents sunburn and glare.

Documentation & Identification

Documents

- Passport/ID in waterproof bag.

Ship's Registry

- May assist in clarifying vessel details post-rescue.

Backup Power

Portable Power Bank

- Recharges communication devices.

Solar Charger

- For extended survival scenarios.

Other Essentials

Spare Clothing

- Warmth after exposure.

Fishing Kit

- Potential food source in prolonged survival.

Bucket/Bailer

- Remove water from life raft, maintain buoyancy.

Notepad/Logbook

- Document events, track time, leave messages.

CHAPTER 66

OPEN-WATER SURVIVAL

Staying Afloat

Use Personal Flotation Devices (PFDs)
- Wear a life jacket properly secured.
- Conserve energy, avoid unnecessary movement.

If No PFD
- Inflate clothing by trapping air or tie off pant/shirt openings.
- Improvise flotation with bottles, debris, seat cushions.

Maintaining Warmth

Protect Against Hypothermia
- Keep head and neck above water; arms close to the body.
- Adopt the HELP position (Heat Escape Lessening Posture).

Use Available Resources

- Layered/insulated clothing, improvised barriers from wind/waves.
- Huddle with others to share body heat.

Managing Energy and Resources

Conserve Energy

- Stay still or float instead of swimming.
- Breathe calmly; avoid panic.

Prevent Dehydration

- Never drink seawater; collect rainwater if possible.
- Ration fresh water supplies carefully.

Signaling for Rescue

Visual Signals

- Flares, mirrors, bright objects held above water.

Audible Signals

- Whistles, horns, or periodic shouting (conserve energy between attempts).

Strategies for Long-Term Survival

- Monitor physical health (hypothermia signs, dehydration).
- Create or maintain a stable floating platform if possible.
- Stay positive, encourage group cooperation if with others.

Chapter 67

WATER AND FOOD SURVIVAL TECHNIQUES

Water Survival

Fresh Water Sources

- Bottled/emergency kit water.
- Rainwater collection (tarps, life jackets, plastic sheets).
- Solar stills or condensation methods if equipment permits.

Avoid Drinking Seawater – accelerates dehydration.

Food Survival

Emergency Rations

- High-calorie bars from raft kits; portion them out.

Fishing/Foraging

- Hooks, lines, lures in the raft kit.
- Improvised gear (shoelaces, sharp objects).

- Carefully consume raw fish/shellfish; avoid unknown species.

Ration Food

- Keep consumption low unless physically active.

Preventing Dehydration

- Stay shaded (raft canopy, clothing).
- Avoid overexertion and unnecessary sweating.
- Collect and store any freshwater as soon as possible.

Mental Strategies

- Stay calm, maintain a survival mindset.
- Use teamwork to collect and ration supplies.
- Monitor for dehydration (fatigue, dizziness) or starvation (weakness, confusion).

Chapter 68

DEALING WITH SHARKS AND MARINE LIFE

Understanding Sharks

- Sharks rarely attack unless provoked or lured by blood/food scents.
- Shiny objects or erratic splashing can attract them.

Shark Survival Techniques

Minimize Attraction

- No blood or fish waste near your area; remove reflective items.
- Move calmly, avoid splashing.

If Approached

- Stay calm, keep the shark in view.
- Defend with oars/poles if aggressive, aiming for eyes/gills.

Dealing with Other Marine Life

Jellyfish
- Avoid contact; rinse stings with seawater, apply vinegar if available.

Stingrays
- Shuffle feet in shallow waters.

Barracudas/Predatory Fish
- Avoid shiny items; remain calm, no sudden splashing.

Safe Practices

- Stay afloat using life jackets/rafts; limit limbs in water.
- Continuously scan surroundings for dorsal fins or unusual fish activity.
- Use flares or improvised tools to repel curious animals.

Managing Marine Life Injuries

Shark Bites – Control bleeding, clean wound, prevent infection.

Jellyfish Stings – Remove tentacles, rinse with seawater.

Cuts/Punctures – Clean with available water, bandage securely.

CHAPTER 69

LONG-TERM RESCUE SCENARIOS

Understanding Long-Term Challenges

- Rescue may take weeks/months; survivors face isolation, limited communication.
- Hunger, exhaustion, and environmental threats increase stress.

Building Mental/Emotional Resilience

- **Acceptance of Reality** – Focus on actionable steps.
- **Short-Term Goals** – Break time into hours or days; routine tasks.
- **Maintaining Hope** – Visualize rescue, practice positive affirmations.
- **Stress Management** – Deep breathing, mindfulness to stay calm.

Coping with Isolation

- **Alone**: Self-talk, journaling, maintaining cognitive clarity.

- **In a Group**: Assign roles, resolve conflicts calmly, support each other.

Emotional Resilience Strategies

- **Constructive Outlets** – Channel emotions through problem-solving.
- **Avoid Despair** – Don't dwell on unknown timeframes; celebrate small wins.
- **Gratitude** – Recognize what resources or positives remain.

Practical Steps to Support Mental Health

- **Physical Activity** – Light exercise or stretching.
- **Nutrition & Hydration** – Balance rationing with minimal consumption for clarity.
- **Communication & Connection** – Open dialogue if with others; keep active in signaling for rescue.

External Stimuli

- **Environment** – Observe surroundings, track weather, spot hazards.
- **Problem-Solving** – Improve shelter, gather resources, create tasks.
- **Creativity** – Invent games, adapt materials, maintain mental engagement.

Signs of Distress & Group Support

- Recognize Apathy, Irritability, Confusion

- Provide reassurance, talk through fears, share hopeful messages.
- Keep focus on the goal of rescue and survival tasks.

Key Takeaways for Chapter 69

- **Acceptance & Hope**: Face reality but maintain optimism.
- **Set Short-Term Goals**: Divide time into manageable segments, create daily routines.
- **Teamwork & Communication**: Support each other, share tasks, resolve conflicts.
- **Psychological Techniques**: Breathing exercises, positive self-talk, celebrate small achievements.

CHAPTER 70

CONSERVING ENERGY AND RESOURCES IN LONG-TERM RESCUE SCENARIOS

Importance of Conserving Energy

Preventing Exhaustion

- Overexertion leads to fatigue, dehydration, and heightened caloric needs.

Maintaining Vital Functions

- Conserving energy allows the body to focus on crucial processes (body heat, muscle function).

Avoiding Overexertion

- Physical activity demands more food and water— resources that are limited.

Techniques to Conserve Energy

a. Limit Physical Activity

- Stay seated/reclined; minimize unnecessary movement.

- Avoid swimming; it rapidly depletes energy and body heat.
- Group tasks (water collection, signaling) to reduce repeated efforts.

b. Maintain a Rest Schedule

- Alternate rest shifts if in a group; one keeps watch while others sleep.
- Sleep whenever possible to preserve physical and mental strength.

c. Protect Against Exposure

- Use canopies, tarps, or clothing to shield from wind, rain, and sun.
- Stay dry; share body heat (huddling) to maintain warmth in cold conditions.

Efficient Resource Management

a. Water Conservation

- Ration water in small sips; avoid large gulps.
- Never drink seawater or contaminated water.
- Capture and store rainwater using tarps, containers, or clothing.

b. Food Conservation

- Ration food into small portions for sustained energy.
- Focus on hydration over eating if supplies are limited.
- Use fishing/foraging only if the energy cost isn't excessive.

c. Resource Recycling

- Reuse containers/clothing for new purposes (water storage, insulation).

- Maintain/repair fishing gear, signaling devices, and other survival tools.

Mental and Strategic Approaches

a. Plan for Long-Term Survival

- Prioritize essentials: water collection, rationing, signaling.
- Break time into manageable intervals to stay focused.

b. Avoid Panic

- Stay calm; fear wastes energy and leads to poor decisions.
- Conserve mental energy by focusing on actionable tasks, not rescue timelines.

Common Mistakes to Avoid

a. Overexertion

- Unnecessary swimming or busywork drains energy reserves quickly.

b. Wasteful Resource Use

- Consuming all water/food too soon cuts long-term survival chances.

c. Exposure to Elements

- Failing to protect from cold/heat/wetness accelerates energy loss.

Key Takeaways for Energy & Resource Conservation

Category	Techniques
Physical Activity	Limit movement, share tasks, focus on essentials
Hydration	Ration water, collect rain, avoid seawater
Nutrition	Ration food, prioritize water, fish/forage wisely
Protection	Use shelter, stay warm/dry, avoid unnecessary exposure
Mental Strategy	Stay calm, set small goals, focus on survival tasks

PART TWELVE

AFTER THE EMERGENCY

Chapter 71

REPORTING INCIDENTS AND LEGAL REQUIREMENTS

Importance of Reporting

- **Safety & Prevention**: Helps authorities analyze causes and improve maritime regulations.
- **Legal Obligations**: Mandatory reporting for accidents involving loss of life, property damage, pollution, etc.
- **Insurance Claims**: Accurate incident reports facilitate claims processing.

Incidents Requiring Reporting

- Collisions, Groundings, Sinking/Capsizing, Injuries/ Fatalities, Fires/Explosions, Pollution.
- Thresholds vary by jurisdiction (e.g., damage above a certain $$ amount, serious injuries).

Reporting Procedures

- **Immediate Notification**: Contact Coast Guard or maritime authority via VHF (Channel 16) or phone.

- **Written Reports**: Submit within the legally mandated timeframe (often 24–48 hours).
- Include vessel/operator info, incident details, damages, injuries.

Legal Requirements

- **International Maritime Law**: IMO protocols for major casualties/pollution in international waters.
- **National Laws**:
  - US: U.S. Coast Guard (Title 33/46 CFR)
  - UK: Maritime & Coastguard Agency (MCA)
  - EU: EMSA regulations
- **Environmental agencies must be notified in case of spills.**

Post-Incident Follow-Up

- Authorities may investigate cause (provide logs, interviews).
- Legal liability may arise from negligence/violations.
- Coordinate with insurance (photos, witness statements, repair estimates).

Tips for Accurate Reporting

- Document events ASAP (photos, notes).
- Be honest, thorough.
- Know your local/regional obligations.

Chapter 72

SHARING LESSONS LEARNED

Importance

- **Enhances Maritime Safety**: Others learn from effective practices & mistakes.
- **Continuous Improvement**: Identifies training/ equipment gaps.
- **Collaborative Culture**: Creates shared knowledge among mariners and authorities.

Key Components of Lessons

- **Root Cause Analysis**: Equipment failure, human error, environment?
- **Effective Practices**: Quick safety gear deployment, strong crew coordination.
- **Challenges Faced**: Inadequate equipment, role confusion, adverse weather.
- **Recommendations**: Drills, upgraded gear, better maintenance schedules.

Methods for Sharing

- **Crew Debriefings**: Team meetings to discuss perspectives, document key points.
- **Reports to Authorities/Organizations**: Coast Guard, industry safety bodies.
- **Internal Communication**: Company reports, incorporate into training modules.
- **Public Forums/Conferences**: Present findings to broader maritime community.

Best Practices

- **Honesty & Transparency**: Include both successes and failures.
- **Clear, Concise Communication**: Organized reporting of key points.
- **Engage Stakeholders**: Crew, management, regulators, and others.

Incorporating Lessons Learned

- **Update Emergency Plans**: Address any protocol weaknesses.
- **Improve Training**: Focus on identified knowledge gaps.
- **Upgrade Equipment**: Replace ineffective tools, improve maintenance.
- **Follow-Up Drills**: Test new procedures.

Example (Fire Onboard)

- Root cause: Faulty wiring in engine room.

- Effective: Quick extinguishing, timely rescue contact.
- Challenges: One extinguisher failed, confusion about evacuation roles.
- Recommendations: Stricter maintenance, regular fire drills, better hazard identification.

Chapter 73

INSPECTING DAMAGE, BOAT REPAIRS AND MAINTENANCE

Initial Safety Measures

- **Personal Safety**: Wear life jackets, gloves; check for fuel leaks/electrical hazards.
- **Stabilize Vessel**: Pump out water, secure anchors to prevent drifting.

Systematic Damage Inspection

- **Hull & Structural Integrity**: Cracks, punctures, warped sections (both above/below waterline).
- **Propulsion System**: Check engine for leaks, propeller alignment, belts, hoses.
- **Electrical System**: Inspect batteries, wiring, radios, lights for shorts or damage.
- **Fuel System**: Look for line leaks, dents in fuel tanks, clogged filters.
- **Safety Equipment**: Life jackets, life rafts, extinguishers, signaling gear.

- **Navigation & Steering**: Rudder or hydraulic steering issues, verify GPS/radar functionality.
- **Environmental Damage**: Oil/fuel in bilge, water intrusion in compartments.

Documenting the Damage

- Take detailed photos/videos of all impacted areas.
- Record exact locations/types of damage; note date/time.
- Maintain a structured checklist for thorough coverage.

Reporting & Follow-Up

- Inform authorities if significant damage or pollution risk.
- File insurance claim with documentation.
- Involve marine surveyors or professionals for critical repairs.

Preventing Further Damage

- **Temporary Repairs**: Apply sealants, patches, duct tape to stabilize until professional fixes.
- **Ongoing Monitoring**: Recheck vessel regularly, especially if conditions change or more leaks appear.

Benefits of Thorough Inspection

- **Safety**: Identifies immediate hazards.
- **Repair Planning**: Helps set priorities for restoration.
- **Insurance Claims**: Ensures faster, more accurate processing.
- **Prevention**: Guides better maintenance and readiness for future incidents.

Chapter 74

PREVENTING FUTURE ISSUES

1. Conduct a Post-Emergency Review

- **Crew Debrief**: Discuss what happened, what went well, and what can improve.
- **Analyze Root Causes**: Investigate equipment failures, human errors, and environmental factors.
- **Document Findings**: Create a detailed report of lessons learned.

2. Improve Vessel Maintenance

- **Regular Inspections**: Check hull, engines, electrical systems for damage or wear.
- **Preventive Maintenance**: Follow manufacturer schedules, replace worn parts, upgrade outdated equipment.
- **Emergency Equipment**: Confirm life jackets, rafts, extinguishers, and radios are functional and ready.

3. Enhance Training and Preparedness

- **Emergency Drills**: Practice evacuation, fire response, and man-overboard scenarios.
- **Skill Development**: Ensure crew familiarity with systems, first aid, and navigational certifications.
- **Scenario Planning**: Simulate potential emergencies for readiness testing.

4. Update Emergency Plans

- **Review & Revise**: Address weaknesses discovered in the incident review.
- **Communication Protocols**: Establish clear procedures for calling authorities/rescue.
- **Accessibility**: Ensure all crew can quickly access and understand emergency documents.

5. Invest in Advanced Safety Systems

- **Modern Navigation Tools**: Use updated GPS, radar, weather monitoring.
- **Redundant Systems**: Backup for steering, propulsion, and communication.
- **Environmental Sensors**: Detect leaks, overheating, or water ingress early.

6. Foster a Safety Culture

- **Encourage Reporting**: Promote a no-blame environment for near-misses/issues.
- **Promote Awareness**: Keep crew informed on safety protocols and new tech.

- **Leadership Commitment**: Demonstrate top-down importance of safety.

7. Monitor and Adapt

- **Track Trends**: Look for patterns in incidents/ maintenance logs.
- **Stay Informed**: Keep up with industry standards/ regulations.
- **Adjust as Needed**: Update procedures, training, and equipment continuously.

8. Summary of Prevention Steps

Category	Actions
Incident Review	Debrief, analyze root causes, document findings
Maintenance	Routine inspections, preventive maintenance, upgrades
Training	Drills, skill dev., certifications
Emergency Plans	Revise protocols, clarify communication, ensure access
Safety Systems	Modern tech, redundancy, sensors
Safety Culture	Reporting environment, leadership emphasis, awareness

Chapter 75

COPING WITH STRESS AND TRAUMA

Understanding Stress and Trauma

- **Stress Response**: May include heightened alertness, difficulty sleeping, irritability.
- **Trauma Effects**: Emotional (fear, guilt), physical (headaches, fatigue), behavioral changes.

Immediate Steps Post-Emergency

- **Ensure Safety**: Stabilize the environment to reduce immediate stress.
- **Rest & Recover**: Replenish energy with food, water, and sleep.
- **Communicate**: Share experiences with others; talking helps process the event.

Coping Mechanisms

- **Acknowledge Emotions**: Accept that fear/sadness/ anger are normal.

- **Stress-Relief Techniques**: Deep breathing, muscle relaxation, mindfulness.
- **Maintain Routine**: A sense of normalcy aids emotional recovery.

Seeking Support

- **Talk to Trusted People**: Friends, family, crew for emotional backing.
- **Professional Help**: Counseling or therapy, support groups, crisis hotlines.
- **Encourage Others**: Promote professional help for those struggling.

Helping Others Cope

- **Emotional Support**: Listen empathetically, reassure.
- **Team Resilience**: Group discussions or activities to process the event collectively.

Recognizing When to Seek Help

- **Persistent Symptoms**: Flashbacks, severe anxiety, depression lasting weeks.
- **Physical Health Concerns**: Chronic insomnia, fatigue, or other issues.

Long-Term Strategies for Mental Health

- **Develop Coping Skills**: Positive thinking, practical problem-solving.

- **Build Emotional Resilience**: Self-care, maintaining social connections.
- **Learn from Experience**: Reflection can lead to stronger preparedness.

Culture of Mental Wellness

- **Training & Preparedness**: Include stress management in crew programs.
- **Regular Check-Ins**: Monitor crew well-being after each voyage.
- **Accessible Resources**: Provide info on counseling or support lines.

Summary of Coping Strategies

Step	Action
Immediate Recovery	Secure safety, rest, communicate feelings
Coping Mechanisms	Relaxation techniques, routine, accept emotions
Seek Support	Family/friends, support groups, professional counseling
Long-Term Health	Develop coping skills, maintain resilience, reflect on lessons

CHAPTER 76

REBUILDING CONFIDENCE ON THE WATER

1. Acknowledge and Process

- **Reflect on the Incident**: Understand causes and outcomes.
- **Recognize Emotions**: Fear, anxiety, hesitation are natural.
- **Talk It Out**: Share with trusted individuals or professionals.

2. Rebuild Skills & Knowledge

- **Training**: Advanced safety courses, updated certifications.
- **Practice Drills**: Fire response, man-overboard, evacuation.
- **Learn New Skills**: Weather forecasting, advanced navigation, vessel maintenance.

3. Take Gradual Steps Back

- **Start Small**: Short, easy trips in calm conditions.

- **Bring Support**: Experienced friends or crew for reassurance.
- **Increase Challenges**: Longer or more difficult voyages as confidence returns.

4. Focus on Preparedness

- **Maintain Vessel**: Thorough inspections and upkeep.
- **Update Emergency Supplies**: Ensure life jackets, extinguishers, radios, etc., are ready.
- **Plan Each Trip**: Float plans, check weather, inform someone ashore.

5. Address Psychological Barriers

- **Manage Fear**: Challenge negative thoughts, use relaxation.
- **Positive Experiences**: Recall enjoyable past trips, celebrate small wins.
- **Professional Support**: Therapy if fears persist.

6. Supportive Community

- **Boating Groups**: Share experiences, learn from others.
- **Group Activities**: Regattas, social sails for confidence-building.
- **Mentors**: Seek out seasoned mariners for advice and guidance.

7. Measure Progress

- **Keep a Journal**: Track milestones and breakthroughs.

- **Reflect on Growth**: Notice improvements in confidence over time.
- **Set Goals**: Plan new challenges to continue building skills.

8. Emphasize Safety & Enjoyment

- **Prioritize Safety**: Confidence grows when you feel secure.
- **Reconnect with Passion**: Focus on the fun and fulfillment of being on the water.

9. Summary of Steps

Step	Action
Process Experience	Reflect on incident, emotions, discuss with others
Rebuild Skills	Training, drills, learn new techniques
Start Small	Gradual approach (calm waters, short trips)
Preparedness	Maintain gear, plan trips, update emergency supplies
Address Anxiety	Relaxation, positive mindset, professional help if needed
Join Community	Boating groups, group sails, supportive mentors

PART THIRTEEN

EMERGENCY CONTACTS

U.S. AND EUROPEAN COAST GUARD, BOATUS, AND SEA TOW

United States

U.S. Coast Guard (USCG)

Emergency Contact: Dial 911 or hail on **VHF Channel 16**.

District Contacts (Command Centers):
- **District 1 (Boston, MA)**: (617) 223-8555
- **District 5 (Portsmouth, VA)**: (757) 398-6231
- **District 7 (Miami, FL)**: (305) 415-6800
- **District 8 (New Orleans, LA)**: (504) 589-6225
- **District 9 (Cleveland, OH)**: (216) 902-6117
- **District 11 (Alameda, CA)**: (510) 437-3701
- **District 13 (Seattle, WA)**: (206) 220-7001
- **District 14 (Honolulu, HI)**: (808) 535-3333
- **District 17 (Juneau, AK)**: (907) 463-2000

Website: U.S. Coast Guard (https://www.uscg.mil/)

BoatUS

Emergency Towing Service:
- Phone (24/7 Dispatch): 800-391-4869
- VHF Radio: Hail "TowBoatUS" on **Channel 16**

Website: BoatUS Towing Services

Sea Tow

Emergency Assistance:
- Phone (24/7 Dispatch): 800-4-SEATOW (800-473-2869)
- VHF Radio: Hail "Sea Tow" on **Channel 16**

Website: Sea Tow Services (https://seatow.com/)

Europe

RNLI (Royal National Lifeboat Institution) – UK & Ireland

Emergency: Dial 999 or 112, ask for Coastguard.

Website: RNLI (https://rnli.org/)

SNSM (Société Nationale de Sauvetage en Mer) – France

Emergency: Dial 196 or use VHF Channel 16.

Website: SNSM (https://www.snsm.org/)

DGzRS (Deutsche Gesellschaft zur Rettung Schiffbrüchiger) – Germany

Emergency: +49 421 536870 or VHF 16.

Website: DGzRS (https://www.dgzrs.de/)

SSRS (Swedish Sea Rescue Society) – Sweden

Emergency: Dial 112 or VHF Channel 16.

Website: SSRS (https://www.sjoraddning.se/)

NSSR (Norwegian Society for Sea Rescue) – Norway

Emergency: Dial 120 or VHF Channel 16.

Website: NSSR (https://www.redningsselskapet.no/)

Sea-Watch – Central Mediterranean
  Website: Sea-Watch

Sea-Eye – Central Mediterranean
  Website: Sea-Eye

Important Notes

- **VHF Channel 16**: International distress frequency, monitored by maritime rescue services.
- **Local Services**: Familiarize with local contacts prior to any voyage.
- **IMO**: For international sea rescue info, refer to International Maritime Rescue Federation.

Air Support for Maritime Emergencies

Air support is crucial for search and rescue (SAR) in ocean rescues. Below are key agencies and resources:

United States

U.S. Coast Guard (USCG)

- Operates aircraft like **MH-60 Jayhawk** & **MH-65 Dolphin** helicopters, **HC-130 Hercules** fixed-wing.
- Contact via **VHF Ch. 16**, phone, or district RCCs (same numbers as above).

Civil Air Patrol (CAP)

- Auxiliary of the U.S. Air Force assists in coastal/ inland SAR.

Canada

CCG & Royal Canadian Air Force (RCAF)

- Coordinates through **Joint Rescue Coordination Centers (JRCCs)**:
  - ○ JRCC Trenton: 1-800-267-7270
  - ○ JRCC Halifax: 1-800-565-1582
  - ○ JRCC Victoria: 1-800-567-5111
- Aircraft include **CH-149 Cormorant** helos, **CC-130 Hercules** planes.

International

GMDSS (Global Maritime Distress and Safety System)

- SAR resources coordinated globally by **IMO**.
- Nearby nations' aircraft are deployed as needed.

NATO & Allied Air Resources

- Nations like France, UK, etc., can deploy aircraft under GMDSS or VHF Ch. 16 requests.

Private Organizations

Air Ambulance & Private Helicopter Charters

- Provide offshore rescues on a contractual/ emergency basis.

How to Request Air Support

- Hail on **VHF Ch. 16**, or use **EPIRB/PLB** signals, or satellite phone.

- Ties in with local RCC or Coast Guard for dispatch.

U.S. Coast Guard (USCG) List by States (including Great Lakes)

Atlantic Ocean States

- **Connecticut** (District 1, Boston): (617) 223-8555
- **Delaware** (District 5, Portsmouth): (757) 398-6231
- **Florida** (District 7, Miami): (305) 415-6800
- **Georgia** (District 7, Miami): (305) 415-6800
- **Maine** (District 1, Boston): (617) 223-8555
- **Maryland** (District 5, Portsmouth): (757) 398-6231
- **Massachusetts** (District 1, Boston): (617) 223-8555
- **New Hampshire** (District 1, Boston): (617) 223-8555
- **New Jersey**
  - ◦ - Northern NJ → District 1: (617) 223-8555
  - ◦ - Southern NJ → District 5: (757) 398-6231
- **New York** (Atlantic) (District 1, Boston): (617) 223-8555
- **North Carolina** (District 5, Portsmouth): (757) 398-6231
- **Rhode Island** (District 1, Boston): (617) 223-8555
- **South Carolina** (District 7, Miami): (305) 415-6800
- **Virginia** (District 5, Portsmouth): (757) 398-6231

Pacific Ocean States

- **Alaska** (District 17, Juneau): (907) 463-2000
- **California** (District 11, Alameda): (510) 437-3701
- **Hawaii** (District 14, Honolulu): (808) 535-3333
- **Oregon** (District 13, Seattle): (206) 220-7001
- **Washington** (District 13, Seattle): (206) 220-7001

Great Lakes States
(District 9, Cleveland, OH): (216) 902-6117

- **Illinois, Indiana, Michigan, Minnesota, New York** (Great Lakes region), **Ohio, Pennsylvania, Wisconsin.**
  - ° (District 9, Cleveland, OH): (216) 902-6117

Specifically for Wisconsin (District 9)

- **Command Center**
  - ° **Phone:** (216) 902-6117
  - ° **Email:** d9publicaffairs@uscg.mil
  - ° **Local Stations:**
    - · Station Milwaukee: (414) 747-7182
    - · Station Sturgeon Bay: (920) 743-3367
    - · Station Green Bay: (920) 434-4882
    - · Station Bayfield: (715) 779-3950
    - · Station Kenosha: (262) 654-7637

Canadian Coast Guard (CCG)
– Great Lakes Region

Great Lakes Sector (Sarnia, ON)

- Phone: 1-519-383-1871 or 1-705-773-4342
- Email: DFO.CCGCentralAtoNGreatLakes-GrandsLacsAalaNCentreGCC.MPO@dfo-mpo.gc.ca

Montréal Ice Centre (Dec–May)

- Phone (Icebreaking Ops): 514-283-2784 (24/7)
- Email: dfo.iceopsgreatlakes.glacesopsgrandslacs.mpo@dfo-mpo.gc.ca
- Phone (Ice Conditions): 514-283-2069
- Email: ssggrandslacs-issgreatlakes@ec.gc.ca

JRCC Trenton (Search & Rescue)

- Phone (Toll-Free): 1-800-267-7270
- Phone (Direct): 613-965-3870

Key Notes

- **VHF Channel 16** – Universal distress frequency.
- **Emergency Numbers** – Keep them on hand (mobile & posted onboard).
- **Local Services** – Know the local SAR or rescue station in your cruising area.
- **Air Support** – USCG, RCAF, or allied nations can deploy helicopters/fixed-wing for major offshore rescues.
- **EPIRBs/PLBs** – Activating these beacons triggers rescue coordination and often leads to air support dispatch.

Always ensure your comms devices (VHF, sat phone, PLB/EPIRB) are operational, and that you have these key contacts accessible before setting out to sea.

Captain Rami Geffner, MD's strong affinity and fondness for the ocean has been a steadfast presence throughout his life. From an early age, Rami accompanied his father on a number of sailing trips, where he fell in love with everything about the sea. He now plans and sets out on his own seafaring adventures and is involved with the local maritime community. Rami holds a bachelor's degree in biology, a master's in human anatomy from Rutgers University, a medical degree from the New Jersey School of Medicine, and as well as multiple degrees in Dermatopathology. Rami continues to practice Dermatology, Dermatopathology and Mohs surgery in Pennsylvania and New Jersey. This is his fourth book.